A.K. Ramanujan's Search for Creativity

A.K. Ramanujan's Poetic Craftsmanship

Dr. Sanjay G. Kulkarni

INDIA · SINGAPORE · MALAYSIA

ISBN 979-8-89699-181-6

First Published 2025

Published by Notion Press Media Pvt Ltd,
#7, Red Cross Road, Egmore, Chennai, Tamil Nadu - 600008

Dedicated to

Shri Gajanan Maharaj, Shegaon

&

My Beloved Parents (Aba & Aai)

Contents

Acknowledgement *7*

About the Book...*9*

Chapter-1   A.K. Ramanujan: Contexts and Conditions....................13

Chapter-2   A.K. Ramanujan's Creative Vision..................................41

Chapter-3   A.K. Ramanujan's Critical Idiom 81

Chapter-4   A.K. Ramanujan's Thematic Concern.........................113

Chapter-5   A.K. Ramanujan's Poetic Craftsmanship 131

Bibliography *145*

About the Author *151*

Acknowledgement

At the outset, I am deeply grateful for the blessings of Lord Gajanan Maharaj, Shegaon, and my parents (Aba & Aai), whose encouragement and support have been a constant source of inspiration throughout this journey.

In an addition I would also wish to express my sincere and earnest gratitude to my respected guide, Dr. I. Venkateswarlu, for his inspiration and guidance in completing my Ph.D. and for helping me bring this book to fruition.

Next, I am profoundly thankful to my respected teacher, Dr. H. G. Kulkarni, for his invaluable assistance and unwavering support in every aspect of my work. His encouragement has been a pillar of strength throughout.

I am also thankful to the college authorities, particularly Hon. Shri Balasahebji Pande (Chairman of ABSS) and Hon. Dr. Sudhir Shivnikar (Principal of N.S.B. College), for their moral support and encouragement. I am grateful to the libraries at N.S.B. College and S.R.T.M.U. Nanded for the resources and assistance they provided during my research.

As a faculty member of the Department of English, I have been greatly supported by my colleagues, Dr. J.S. Masure and Dr. Sandeep Kale, who have been a constant source of guidance and collaboration.

I must also express my deep appreciation to my dear friend, Dr. Vitthal Gore, whose help was instrumental in the initial stages of writing this book. His support was crucial in ensuring the project's success from start to finish.

I am thankful to Notion Press for their guidance and support in the publication process, helping me bring this book to its best possible form.

Lastly, but by no means least, I would like to express my honest indebtedness to my family, especially my life partner, Mrs. Pranita, for her unwavering support, love, and encouragement. Without her, completing this work would not have been possible.

About the Book

The principal objective of writing this book and conducting the present study titled "A. K. Ramanujan: A Critical Study" was to analyse his work critically. It aims to highlight various aspects of his poetry, as well as his autobiographical and reflective nature. An effort has also been made to present him as a true Indian expatriate poet and a Hindu, from both his literary and personal perspectives.

A review of his contributions, an assessment of Indo-Anglian poetry, and his vision of life as a literary figure have been undertaken to explore his place within the Indo-English poetic landscape. His keen interest in Indian-ness, as a truly Indian poet in an expatriate condition, compels us to study the significance of his poetic work from the viewpoints of both a critic and a researcher.

The book as titled is a modest attempt to highlight the remarkable work undertaken by major poets, such as A. K. Ramanujan, in Indian Writing in English. The aim of this study is to review the various techniques these poets employ to convey their vision of life focusing more on A. K. Ramanujan's contributions.

It also reflects the distinctive features of their poetry, including the symbolic significance of their work, mood, tone, and technical strategies, while characterizing Indian English poetry today. Additionally, this effort seeks to explore patterns of self-exploration and the diverse approaches of these poets as new voices in literature.

The book design follows an explorative, interpretative, and descriptive model. A Critical Study is undertaken to uncover the complexities and layers of meaning in his work. It also assesses his Indian identity and work from various perspectives, such as psychological, nostalgic, existential, social, cultural, aesthetic, and more. Therefore, this book makes a modest attempt to focus on A. K. Ramanujan, his place, and the insights with autobiographical elements in his poetry. It explores the conceptual design and expressive modes that emerge in his work, aiming to exemplify and evaluate him in an indigenous context.

While many critics and distinguished scholars have directed their views towards the interpretation and revaluation of contemporary Indian poetry in English, the poetry of major poets like A. K. Ramanujan has not been specifically addressed. Thus, the motivation for this writing is to study and evaluate his literary contributions by reviewing his relatively small body of work.

His long stay in the United States undoubtedly gave a new orientation to his outlook and even to his roots in his native Indian culture, particularly in his Hindu heritage. However, this was a gain, not a loss, even though he was a voluntary exile from India and distanced himself from his immediate Hindu native environment.

The key question is how his enterprising nature and Indian sensibility enabled him to engage with India's past. How was his understanding of Indian history and tradition unique? How can it be said that he achieved a remarkable breakthrough in cross-fertilizing English with native literary traditions?

No doubt, this is possible due to his being a polyglot writer, a critic, and a literary figure. However, the principal reasons behind the attention his work has received from critics both in India and abroad need to be explored. Why have so many critics paid special attention to his poetry? Why was he historically important for the study of post-independence Indian English poetry? What makes his poetic character unique? How does he demonstrate his respect for the craft, making his poetry more than just a mere expression of emotion or idea? How is his art almost always perfect and finely nuanced? Why is it commendable, regardless of what he has to his credit? Why do we acclaim him and recognize his established position as one of the most talented 'new poets'?

Furthermore, a careful reading of his poetry, from his first volume to his last, reveals that he gave equal importance to both his creative and translated works. More importantly, how is his poetry in English inspired by a sensibility that is both distinctly Indian and Western in a unique way? Finally, how can we authentically accept his Indian sensibility and present his poetry in a balanced perspective, aiming to clarify and evaluate him as a poet and his poetic works?

To sum up, the present writing aims to explore the significance of the titled book and its principal reasons. In short, it seeks to affirm why Ramanujan is poetically unique, why his poetry deserves special attention, and how each chapter is concluded in an objective manner. Additionally, the scheme for discerning the chapter structure is a modest effort to evaluate and analyse the titled book. However, the emphasis is on clarification and evaluation. The work offers six chapters, each representing his expression of experience in exploration.

CHAPTER-1

A.K. Ramanujan: Contexts and Conditions

Indo-English poetry has gained international recognition today. A comprehensive survey of its entire body of work is beyond the scope of this chapter. Therefore, this assessment of Indo-English poetry, along with its background, represents a small effort to study it in next sections. To properly assess Indo-English poetry, one must consider the following points: 1) Introduction: A Review, 2) Pre-Independence Poets and Poetry: An Introduction, 3) Post-Independence Poets and Poetry: An Introduction, 4) Major Aspects and Themes in Pre-Independence Poetry, and 5) Major Aspects and Themes in Post-Independence Poetry.

In reviewing Indo-English poetry, one must look at all the aspects of its development from the beginning. Indian poets have been writing poetry in English for over a century and a half, and it is natural that critical attempts have been made from time to time to assess their significant contributions. This has helped to build a new tradition of poetry through an alien medium, which has captivated the imagination through its poetic beauty and flexibility.

A noted writer in Indo-English poetry, S. Z. H. Abidi, writes, **"The story of the growth and development of Indo-Anglian poetry is one of tradition, experiment, imitation, and innovation."** (1996, Prakash Book Depot, p. 1). This suggests that a tradition may have a beginning, but it has no end.

The first poetry in English written by Indian poets can be traced down from 1839. To elaborate, this tradition began with Henry Derozio (1807–1831), but as it has evolved into an on-going line of poetic exploration, the tradition in Indo-English poetry was laid down and enriched by individual poets, both major and minor, from 1828 to 1950.

The outstanding contributions of some of these poets became famous in India and abroad due to their poetic merit and considerable skill in the use of imagery and poetic techniques. Others, while notable for their curiosity, value and historical significance, may not have achieved the same level of repute. Among these poets, A. K. Ramanujan stands out as a major figure whose work deserves special consideration.

To explore and comprehend the poetry of the Pre-Independence period, it is essential to review the poets who helped to make Indian poetry in English acceptable to a broad audience, both in India and abroad. Key figures from the early phase of Indo-English poetry include Henry Derozio (1807–1831), Michael Madhusudan Dutt (1824–1873), Toru Dutt (1856–1877), Manmohan Ghose (1824–1924), Sri Aurobindo (1872–1950), Rabindranath Tagore (1861–1941), Sarojini Naidu (1879–1949), and many others.

The real beginning of Indian poetry in English came into existence when Henry Derozio published his first poem, *The Fakir of Jungheera*, in 1828. As S. Z. H. Abidi rightly notes, the use of English as a creative medium during British rule in India was a consequence of the historical situation.

Indo-English poetry reached a significant milestone when Macaulay introduced English education in India in 1835, setting the stage for its permanent place in Indian literary tradition. The major poets of the Pre-Independence period laid the foundation of Indian English verse with their exceptional poetic gifts and individual talents. As S. Z. H. Abidi comments, "It became non-derivative and authentic by their hand only." (1996, Prakash Book Depot, p. 2).

H. L. V. Derozio, the first Indo-Anglian poet, is known for his remarkable 'historicity.' His poem *The Fakir of Jungheera* (1828) marks the first important milestone in the development of Indo-Anglian poetry. In his poem *The Harp of India*, Derozio expresses his love for his motherland, while in *To India* and *My Native Land*, he sings of India's past glory.

After Derozio (1807–1831), Michael Madhusudan Dutt (1824–1873) made significant contributions to Indo-English poetry. He initially wrote his poems in English before switching to Bengali, his native language. Among his notable works are *King Porus – A Legend* and *The Captive Lady* (1849).

Similarly, Toru Dutt was a pioneering figure in Indo-Anglian poetry, known for her historical position and innovation. Her ballads reflect her poetic worth and her deep connection to Indian culture and religion. Although she lived only for twenty-one years, her poetry remains a testament to her authentic Indian-ness and cultural emphasis.

Many poets, critics, and poet-critics have expressed reservations about using Aurobindo's poetry in contemporary discussions. However, their critiques often fail to acknowledge the originality and depth of his work. Aurobindo's shorter lyrics, sonnets, and narrative poems, which deal with Indian myths and historical events, demonstrate a fresh approach and a genuine attempt at original interpretation. His epic poem *Savitri* captures the spirit of the Upanishadic Movement, establishing him as a prominent figure in both Indian and global literary circles. Aurobindo's work during (1890–1950) firmly places him as a Commonwealth writer and an Indian Yogi.

Another important figure who gained immense popularity in the history of India's struggle for independence and in Indo-Anglian poetry was **Sarojini Naidu**. She was a recipient of the *Kaiser-i-Hind* medal and a gold medal for her poetry. She was also a fellow of the Royal Society of Literature. As a poet, she shared similarities with **Manmohan Ghose**. Both wrote primarily on themes of love, nature, death, and pain, and both belonged to the **Elizabethan school of lyricism**. Sarojini Naidu's poetry was sensuous, romantic, and lyrical. In one of her poems, she praises **Mother India**. Her major works include the volumes *The Golden Threshold* (1905), *The Bird of Time* (1912), and *The Broken Wing* (1917).

Towards the end of the colonial era, Indian poetry in English became distinctly Indian in both subject matter and style, reflecting the country's culture, beliefs, customs, and social realities. Poets like **Toru Dutt**, with her romantic poetry and Indian mysticism, and **Sarojini Naidu**, with her nationalist poem *Bengal Sellers*, consciously embraced Indian themes. In short, early poetry in English was genuinely Indian, and these poets worked to present India to the world.

Before India's independence, the poetry of most Indian poets was driven by a sense of identity – whether in terms of religion, culture, or the quest for self-definition. The major concern of these poets was to examine the search for self and define its contexts and dimensions. They also sought to explore their personalities and insights, often through autobiographical elements in their works. Poets like **Lokmanya Tilak, V. D. Savarkar, Sri Aurobindo, Rabindranath Tagore**, and **Sarojini Naidu** sang the spirit of *Mother India*. Their poetry, full of patriotic fervour, aimed to awaken Indians to their collective strength and cultural heritage.

To understand the poetry of the Post-Independence period, one must also consider the literature of that era, beginning from the late nineteenth century. The poets of this time, including **Henry Derozio, Madhusudan Dutt, Aurobindo Ghose, Toru Dutt, Sarojini Naidu,** and **Rabindranath Tagore**, were all deeply connected to their Indian roots. Their works not only reflect their cultural heritage but also explore the notion of 'Indian-ness.' This concept became central to the evolution of Indian poetry in English, marking its flowering after independence, alongside poetry written in India's regional languages.

According to R. Parthasarathy, "Indian Independence in 1947 ushered in a period of prosperity in all walks of life[3]" (1993, Oxford University Press, p. 19). He also notes the changes in literature after Independence, pointing out that more and more Indian poets began writing in English. Both major and minor poets sought to give this new poetry a fresh direction, one that would increasingly express more personal and private concerns. The outstanding contributions of Nissim Ezekiel and P. Lal placed them above all others. Not only did they strive to bring attention to this body of poetry, but they also wrote significant verses and anthologies.

Before the 1960s, several Indian poets attempted to give a new direction to their poetry, but only a few succeeded in doing so. Among the most notable were Nissim Ezekiel and P. Lal. In 1960, the Writers' Workshop published only three volumes of poetry and an anthology, a significant honour for any poet or writer associated with the workshop. The Writers' Workshop in Calcutta also issued a poetic manifesto, which summarized the aims, objectives, and challenges of contemporary Indian English poetry.

The first poet to be honoured by this workshop was Nissim Ezekiel, for his well-known three volumes: *The Third*, *Sixty Poems*, and *A Time to Change*. In addition, P. Lal collaborated with K. Raghavendra Rao to write *Modern Indo-English Poetry*.

It seems that only after the 1960s did true modern Indian English poetry begin to emerge, poetry that could be read with both profit and pleasure. The literary contributions of modern Indian English poets reflect the colours of modernity, variety, and superb craftsmanship. This period is also characterized by experimentation, innovation, new imagery, a realistic attitude, and authentic creative expression. In conclusion, S. Z. H. Abidi observes, "Serious Indian poetry is in Indian urge and equally in superb craftsmanship." (1996, Prakash Book Depot, p. 11)

In addition, modern Indian poets in English were inspired by their new faith in the English language as a creative medium. They affirm that their choice of English as a medium for remarkable expression is both free and natural. As an example, P. K. J. Kurup notes that the Indian poets in English of the post-Independence era are poets of transition, standing at the threshold of a literary renaissance and a grand awakening to the possibilities of a new medium. Their ethos is radically different from that of earlier periods.

Thus, after the 1960s, Indian poetry in English underwent a transformation, both in terms of its themes and techniques. To illustrate this, Bijay Kumar Das identifies two kinds of poetry: 'direct poetry', in which the meaning is explicitly stated, and 'oblique poetry', in which the usual approach juxtaposes images and symbols, allowing the reader to draw implicit connections on their own.

He also mentions that he has cited the works of many poets, and there is relatively a formidable list. The major poets in modern Indian English poetry include Nissim Ezekiel, Jayant Mahapatra, A. K. Ramanujan, R. Parthasarathy, Shiv K. Kumar, Keki N. Daruwalla, O. P. Bhatnagar, A. K. Mehrotra, Kamala Das, Gauri Deshpande, Gauri Pant, Lila Ray, Monika Verma, Arun Kolatkar, Gieve Patel, and Margaret Chatterjee. These poets not only expressed new ideas but also presented them in ways quite different from their predecessors.

In other words, these poets "brought innovations in form, imagery, style, structure, and employed a new kind of diction, akin to colloquial language and rhythm" (R. Parthasarathy, 1993, Prakash Book Depot, p. 20), as Dr. B. K. Das rightly observes.

Dr. Das also affirms that some of the modern Indian English poets are close to being called confessional poets, although their confessional tone is more of a strategy than a reality. He further states that before 1960, the techniques adopted in Indian English poetry were, to a large extent, imitative and derivative – historically imperative. This means that the poet should possess the genius to discover a new voice for their new mind, by intimately capturing the idiom of their own world.

A kind of mannerism developed by Indian poets in spoken form, and post-1960s Indian poets in English consistently tried to approximate the rhythm of speech in their poetry. According to Dr. Das, these poets followed the forms of speech and aimed to recreate a vivid and authentic representation of Indian characters and situations. The primary intention behind employing this technique was to capture the spirit of the personages in their natural form, thereby ensuring the reader's total engagement. In other words, this technique sought to create new Indian English idioms, as Nissim Ezekiel had done in his work.

In addition, the use of language is a marked feature of the new technique adopted by post-1960s Indian English poets. Kamala Das, for instance, employed an elliptical style, while O. P. Bhatnagar, R. Parthasarathy, and A. K. Ramanujan used a sonorous style. Nissim Ezekiel, Jayant Mahapatra, and Keki N. Daruwalla employed a vigorous and deeply engaging style, while Gauri Deshpande, Gauri Pant, Lila Ray, and Monika Verma are known for their emotive style. The impressionistic style of Shiv K. Kumar is another distinctive feature of his individual poetic technique. However, very few poets were solely obsessed with the perfection of language. Among them, only Shiv K. Kumar's use of language truly reflects the stamp of his professional style and scholarly learning.

Finally, when evaluating the Post-Independence period, it can be said that only A. K. Ramanujan and R. Parthasarathy were deeply concerned with the perfection of language. To some extent, Daruwalla and Nissim Ezekiel also strove to approximate spoken language. However, it was only Nissim Ezekiel who believed in revising a poem endlessly until it reached the level of perfection he desired.

Other poets, especially women poets, seemed to align with Kamala Das's diction. Thus, these poets express themselves in the most convincing manner using free verse and communicate their experiences through flexible syntax and a new idiomatic style of language. This approach gives rise to the hope of creating a new Indian English idiom. Therefore, this study of post-Independence poetry has a broad perspective, aiming to explore and identify new Indian idiomatic styles.

A broad survey of post-Independence poetry introduces us to the major poets of that period. Many pioneers made outstanding poetic contributions that brought fame to Indian literature in English, both in India and abroad. Among them, four stand out: Nissim Ezekiel, Kamala Das, R. Parthasarathy, and A. K. Ramanujan. These poets published their work in the 1960s, a pivotal decade marking the departure from the old to the new.

In general, their poetry shares common features that distinguish modern Indian poetry in English. The elements that bind Indian poets in English after Independence together are themes, attitudes, form, and language. The wide variety of mood, tone, and technical strategies in their work has shaped the current landscape of Indian English poetry.

The second most important thematic concern of these poets was their varied approach to exploring the self. The vitality in their works lies in their sense of contemporaneity and their conscious effort to be true to their times.

Nissim Ezekiel (1924–2004) was the first poet to undertake the task of capturing the spirit of characters in their natural form, thereby achieving the reader's full participation. His goal in employing his unique technique was to create a new Indian English idiom. In this respect, he is comparable to Chaucer in the realm of modern Indian English poetry, making an outstanding contribution through his writings. He also mentored and encouraged other Indian English poets, such as Dom Moraes and Jayanta Mahapatra. Ezekiel was the only Indian English poet who was equally proficient in both metrical verse and free verse. He also explored a wide range of subjects in his poetry, demonstrating great success in recreating characters within their own situations.

According to Dr. B. K. Das, "His poetry has a sense of immediacy that immediately arrests the attention of the reader, but his irony and humour are the hallmark of his poetry." (Parthasarathy, R., 1993, Oxford University Press, p. 1)

Although he was primarily a poet, Ezekiel's interests were not limited to poetry alone. Dr. Raghukul Tilak writes about Ezekiel: "He was also a great critic by virtue of both the quality and quantity of his criticism" (Tilak, R., 2001, p. 8). Ezekiel wrote three plays –*Nalini*, *The Sleep Walkers*, and *Song of Deprivation* – to his credit. As a poet of the mind, he displayed a marked tendency to explore the human psyche. His poems reveal not only the conscious but also the subconscious thoughts and conflicts of human beings, particularly his own. Indeed, his primary concern was with man and mankind.

Similarly, Nissim Ezekiel demonstrated his genius in infusing his poetry with a rich sense of humour, wit, and irony. His primary weapon of expression is irony. His love poems often focus on the physical and sexual relationships between men and women. The theme of love in these poems revolves around sensuality and lust, rather than true love. Although some of his poems may seem loose in structure, the majority of his work reflects a deep sense of form and structure, along with a special attention to using the right words in the right places.

Following this, Kamala Das devoted herself to making a literary contribution through what she called her 'mine language.' She was one of the key figures in the Indo-Anglian poetic tradition, alongside A. K. Ramanujan and Nissim Ezekiel. Her poetry is deeply personal, focusing on her own intense longing for love, emotional involvement, and her struggles to achieve such relationships.

Thus, knowledge of her life and personality is essential for understanding her poetry. Her real name was Madhavi Kutty, and she was largely educated at home. It is notable that she came from an orthodox and conservative family, yet her poetry is largely unorthodox and almost revolutionary, especially in contrast to the environment in which she was raised.

Kamala Das began writing poetry at an early age, but before she became known in Indo-English poetry, she made a mark in Malayalam literature, publishing eleven books in the language. The Sahitya Akademi honoured her for her work *Tanuppu* in Malayalam. During her extended stays in cities like Calcutta, Bombay, and Delhi, she unconsciously absorbed the influence of working in metropolitan India, and later settled in Trivandrum, Kerala. Her poetry is often labelled 'confessional' because it records her personal experiences, particularly in the realms of marriage and sex. She married at the age of fifteen, but her marriage was an absolute failure.

Her poetry is collected in four volumes: *Summer in Calcutta* (1965), *The Descendants* (1967), *The Old Playhouse and Other Poems* (1978), and *Stranger's Time* (1973). She also wrote her autobiography, titled *My Story* (1975). Kamala Das distinguished herself as an Indo-Anglian poet with an extraordinary command over the English language, and she also achieved prominence as a short story writer in Malayalam. In recognition of her work, the Kerala Sahitya Akademi honoured her with an award in 1969.

Kamala Das expressed bold and controversial views in her essays, which, like her poetry, have made her a polarizing figure. Titles such as *I Studied All Men, Why Not More Than One Husband?* and *I Have Lived Beautifully* reflects her unapologetic stance on various issues. As a poet, Kamala Das is an original voice with a distinctive poetic personality. At her best, she remains unequalled and matchless, but at times she fails to exercise the artistic self-control that marks the height of her work.

The next poet to consider, alongside A. K. Ramanujan, is R. Parthasarathy. Apart from both being southern expatriate writers, they share a preoccupation with familial and cultural heritage, often writing poetry that is personal, reminiscent, and confessional. However, Parthasarathy's expatriate experience differed significantly from Ramanujan's. His first visit to England in 1963, on a scholarship from the British Council, left him deeply disillusioned, as his poetic and lyrical expectations were deflated. Having felt uneasy in India, he found Indian society neurotic and chained to an exaggerated past. He went to England with high hopes, only to encounter disappointment.

This so-called 'disenchantment' with England ultimately helped R. Parthasarathy discover a new understanding of both himself and India. Upon returning to India, he hoped to fully identify with his homeland but found that his ten years of experience as a poet writing in English had alienated him from his own culture and civilization. At the same time, he realized that he would never fully master the English language or feel completely at home in it. He reflects this predicament in his poem 'Tamil.' Disappointment, indeed, becomes the central theme of Parthasarathy's work. He accepts this disappointment, acknowledging his failure to find a tradition in which he could fully immerse himself as a poet.

Despite this, Parthasarathy has a deep admiration for Ramanujan's poetry, particularly the way Ramanujan has used his memories of growing up in a South Indian Brahmin family, with its intricate web of relationships, to capture key aspects of Tamil culture.

The final major poet to consider is A. K. Ramanujan. Ramanujan turned his bilingual background into strength, developing a unique language to express both his personal experiences and the insights he gained from his studies of Tamil and Kannada literatures. In contrast, Parthasarathy still finds himself caught in a dilemma, even contemplating abandoning English altogether and shifting to Tamil. However, inspired by Ramanujan, Parthasarathy sought to establish a relationship between his Indian English poetry and Tamil poetry, attempting to reconcile these two linguistic and cultural worlds.

The need for a brief discussion of the themes explored by early Indian English poets arises from the fact that many thoughtless judgments and easy generalizations have been made in this regard. In truth, their poetry often drew inspiration from the Indian landscape, rural scenes, and from Indian history, mythology, or folklore.

If we examine the poetry of Sri Aurobindo, Toru Dutt, Rabindranath Tagore, and Sarojini Naidu, and other poets who emerged during the nineteenth century and continued writing into the early decades of the twentieth century, we can see a significant contribution to the development of Indian English poetry. However, not all of them warrant serious critical attention, except for historical reasons.

Among the pioneers, Kashiprasad Ghose was the first Indian to publish poetry in English. The kind of poetry produced by him and his followers was, by and large, imitative and derivative, with little claim to originality or innovation. Ghose studied English prosody and criticism under the guidance of his British teacher, who influenced him and shaped his style, which was largely based on the works of Cavalier Poets, Neo-Classical Poets, and Romantic poets. Ghose published his first collection, *The Minstrel and Other Poems*, in 1830. At best, he remains a minor poet, along with his later colleagues such as Rajnarain Dutt.

Indian poetry in English is often said to have begun with a few talented young men, like Henry Derozio, who inspired his pupils with a great love for the language and literature of England. One of his most famous poems is *The Fakir of Jungheera*, a narrative poem that tells the story of how the Brahmin widow Nalini is given a fresh lease on life when she is rescued from being burned alive on the funeral pyre.

Derozio wrote a number of sonnets and short lyrics, with his *best friend* proclaiming his victory over fate. His most celebrated sonnet, *The Harp of India*, uses the image of a harp that now lies lonely and abandoned, bound by silence in its 'fatal silence.' The harp symbolizes India and the nation's poetic or artistic genius. In another poem, *Song of the Hindustani Minstrel*, he presents the beautiful image of a 'Cashmere girl.'

Michael Madhusudan Dutt's reputation as a far more gifted poet rests on his celebrated Bengali epic *Meghnada-Bandha* and his narrative poem *The Captive Lady*, both of which mark significant contributions to the Indian English literary scene. To present the biblical theme of innocence, temptation, and the fall of man, he wrote a collection of verses entitled *Visions of the Past*. His adaptation of the Indian epic is another noteworthy achievement. Though Dutt was highly imaginative, efficient, and a skilled versifier, he falls short as a poet in the broader sense.

Nevertheless, to some extent, his *The Captive Lady*, a narrative poem, proves that he could be a great poet. The poem tells the love story of Prithviraj and Samyukta, where King Prithviraj abducts the daughter of the King of Kannauj. Ultimately, the king and queen kill themselves on a funeral pyre – a dramatic but historically inaccurate conclusion, as Prithviraj was actually killed by his Muslim conquerors. Despite this historical inaccuracy, the poem had far-reaching consequences in Indian literary and cultural history.

Subsequently, Toru Dutt successfully 'Indianized' her idiom in English, despite living for a short period of time. She was also the first Indian poet to place her country on the international literary map. While she had a fondness for France and England, she never lost touch with her roots in India. Her use of French, English, and Sanskrit helped interpret the soul of India to a global audience. Her assertive nature and her zeal to present both nationhood and individuality made her one of the most illustrious daughters of her country.

Toru Dutt's solid achievements laid the foundation for the development of Indo-Anglian literature. Her powerful interpretation of the soul of India for Western audiences, acting as a bridge between the East and the West, established her as the first major poet in Indo-Anglian poetry.

Her fame earned her the title of the 'prestigious child of our country.' Though she was also a novelist, essayist, letter writer, and translator, her true legacy lies in her poetry. *Ancient Ballads* is a collection deeply rooted in Indian themes and treatment. As King Fisher rightly observes, Toru Dutt is remembered more for her poetry than her prose.

The central theme of her novels is love, and the plot often moves through tragedy and suffering. Her well-known volumes, *Ancient Ballads* and *Legends of Hindustani*, are of permanent literary value.

Toru Dutt was highly sensitive to nature, sound, and colour. Her commentary on men, women, and their manners, as well as her sketches of Indian social life, demonstrate her sharp faculty of observation. Her poetry is essentially reflective of her race and her land. She skilfully interpreted the culture, mythology, and Hindu legends of India to foreign audiences. Thus, we can say that Toru Dutt was one of the 'modern' poets, drawing on the popular tales and myths of her past to enrich her poetry. *Ancient Ballads* reflects her deep background in Sanskrit and showcases her poetic heritage.

To conclude, Toru Dutt's poetic diction is mostly simple and clear, with both theme and context clearly articulated. In this regard, she appears more natural than Sarojini Naidu, as both poets had somewhat different attitudes towards nature and humankind. Her letters provide a true and complete picture of her hopes, aspirations, and daily life. They also reveal her scholarly bent of mind. Through her letters, we see how deeply affectionate she was toward her friends, relatives, and acquaintances, offering her kindness and warmth without question.

Similarly, Sri Aurobindo was another undeniably outstanding figure in Indo-Anglian literature. He was widely known as a social thinker, philosopher, prophet, and a distinguished man of letters. His life was shaped by three main pursuits: literature, yoga, and politics. His poetic achievements include a wide range of works, such as lyrics, five plays, two narrative poems, and his magnum opus, *Savitri*.

Aurobindo's poems cover a broad spectrum of subjects, from sensual love to spiritual illumination, all bearing the imprint of a master poet. His immense imagination, command over language, and skilful handling of traditional English metrical forms elevated him to the status of an outstanding poet. Among his greatest contributions to Indian English literature is *Savitri*, an epic poem. In this work, the concluding part of Canto I, 'Fate' in the 'Book of Fate,' forms the central theme. What is significant in this context is that Savitri, the protagonist, believes she is on Earth to fulfil God's divine mission.

Like Aurobindo, Rabindranath Tagore is another highly gifted poet, dramatist, short story writer, and composer. He serves as a bridge between the East and the West and shares the internationalism of figures like Romain Rolland. The entirety of Tagore's work explores the relationship between the finite and the infinite. Like Manmohan Ghose, he was also a lyric poet and, like Sri Aurobindo, a prolific writer.

His *Gitanjali* – a collection of lyrics on God, man, and nature – draws heavily from his personal life. It is the creation of an artist, reflecting his mind and personality. His life, both personal and emotional, was shaped by numerous episodes, readings, and literary influences. *Gitanjali* is a series of songs offered to the creator, with its poetry delving into themes of love, mystical yearning for God, a love for the natural world, and the Endemic world of children.

Love is the central theme in Tagore's poetry, which makes him a great romantic poet, a mystic poet, and, above all, a great lyricist. His treatment of nature reveals his immense and sensuously passionate love for it. Like Wordsworth, Tagore believed that nature and God are one and the same.

One of the most appealing aspects of Tagore's poetry is the beauty and richness of the imagery he employs in his lyrics. His imagery is pervasive and unifying, giving his poems a sense of coherence and depth. Ultimately, love has been the most inspiring theme of his poetry, but his major subjects include love, nature, man, God, and death. As a poet of humanity, he conveys a message of peace, love, and joy. His poetry reflects his religious sentiments and his spiritual connection to the divine.

Lastly, the 'Indian-ness' of Tagore is an open secret. His poetic ideas, sentiments, imagery, and philosophy are deeply rooted in Indian culture and thought.

A notable figure following Tagore is Sarojini Naidu. In her poem 'Indian Weavers,' she depicts India as a land that embodies multiple coexisting cultures – Hindu, Christian, and Mughal. Other aspects of her poetry include her passionate love for beauty, nature, lyricism, mysticism, and philosophy. These qualities bring her close to the English Romantics, particularly Keats and Wordsworth, who also celebrated beauty, nature, and the profound mysteries of life.

The sense of loneliness that haunts the human soul all characteristically is Indian. A close study of her poems like 'Coromandel Fishers' and 'Indian Weavers' leaves us convinced that the real strength of Sarojini's poetry lies in the Indian-ness of the poet's mind and sensibility.

Known as 'Bharat Kokila' or the Nightingale of India, Sarojini Naidu is the most lyrical woman poet of India. Of all the Indo-English poets, she is, perhaps, the most popular both in India and outside. Her chief work is contained in *Golden Threshold* (1905), and almost all her poems present a poetic view imbued with idealism and romanticism. She had an inborn talent for poetry and was nurtured on romantic poetry, English, Persian, and Urdu. Like other poets, she was under the profound influence of Keats, Swinburne, and Tagore, and her verses had a romantic colouring.

Hence, she is called a great music maker with superior poetic craftsmanship. She appeals to our senses through her sensuous romantic poetry. W. B. Yeats called her a 'pure-romantic.' She was a poet by temperament, inclination, and choice. That is why her lyrics are soft and delicate, marked by naturalness and spontaneity.

Sarojini Naidu enjoyed immense popularity both in Indo-Anglian poetry and in the history of the Indian struggle for Independence. She is superior to Toru Dutt and Harin in poetic craftsmanship, and while her themes are not varied, her art is superb. The richness of poetic details, romantic and lyrical quality, gives her poetry freshness and beauty. A sensitive soul, she expresses her response in imagery that heightens our concept of imagination. We remember her for a long time for her image-making capacity and her place in the annals of Indian history as the Nightingale of India.

Hence, music is the soul of her poetry. In many of her poems, as we have seen, she presents Islamic pictures of life and the Hindu gods and goddesses. But everywhere her themes are timeless – love, death, nature, optimism, challenge to fate, and haunting pathos. The desire for beauty made her a poet, and there is beauty in her verses.

To end, we may say, in the light of some of these considerations, that from an Indian point of view, the poetry of Aurobindo, Tagore, and Sarojini Naidu was truly in the indigenous tradition. With all their shortcomings and imperfections, these poets have shown a visionary quality, a preoccupation with the larger questions of life, death, and liberation, which brings them closer to the ancient Indian literary, intellectual, mystical, and spiritual tradition. Thus, in his *Twenty-Five Indian Poets in English*, K. S. Ramamurti rightly affirms that the earlier poets had followed the romantics and the Pre-Raphaelitism.

The poets of the post-Independence period have followed the footsteps of T.S. Eliot, Ezra Pound, and later W.B. Yeats, W.H. Auden, Wallace Stevens, Tom Gunn, and Dylan Thomas. One does not find in their poetry echoes, resonances, and reverberations from the poetry of

Eliot and others. To prove them distinctively Indian, poetry in English and Indian writing in English have drawn themes and ideas from the Vedas, the Upanishads, the Ramayana, and the Mahabharata.

To show the awareness of a worldview that is more Indian than Western in his poetry, Nissim Ezekiel just believes, but does not have his roots in Indian culture and literary tradition. Poets like A. K. Ramanujan, Arun Kolhatkar, Dilip Chitre, and Kamla Das were always involved in developing regional language poetry and translations from their own languages into English to establish an indigenous tradition of Indian English verse. They made this impossible possible by rejecting the romantic, Victorian tradition, but at the same time, they gave worthwhile respect to poets like Eliot, Pound, etc.

It was a significant milestone in the literary ethos of Indian writing in English when poets like Nissim Ezekiel first depicted an urban sensibility and the problems of an emerging city. Similarly, modern Indian poetry in English began with the establishment of the Writer's Workshop in Calcutta, founded and edited by P. Lal and K. Raghavendra Rao in 1958.

As Bruce King writes in his book *Modern Indian Poetry in English* (1987), many of the new poets do not have their roots in a culture that can be considered purely Indian. Very few were born and brought up in Hindu Vaishnava families, such as A. K. Ramanujan and R. Parthasarathy. Some of them came from modernizing or reformist Hindu groups. Ezekiel's parents were Jewish, and Dilip Chitre's family was agnostic but of Hindu descent. Daruwalla, Patel, and Adil Jussawalla belong to the Parsi Zoroastrian community, while Agha Shahid Ali, Saleem Peeradina, and Keshav Malik's parents were from Islamic families. Jayant Mahapatra and Deba Patnaik are Christian converts, and Shiv K. Kumar is a rebel against Hinduism.

Though some of these poets lived in countries like the United States, far away from their native India – by choice or by fate – they never forget their cultural heritage, which is essentially Indian and Hindu.

To conclude, we recognize the poetry of these new poets because they are authentically Indian, representing a composite character of Indian culture, reflecting the variety and changing patterns of values and sensibility in the contemporary literary ethos.

Thus, post-Independence poets reflect the real poetry of the Indian socio-cultural situation, focusing more on urban and metropolitan life rather than the rural India. It is with these poets that Indian English poetry may be said to have entered a new phase.

As Dr. K. R. S. Iyengar rightly affirms, "The emergence of the 'new poetry' in Indian English literature was like its emergence in England, France, and the U.S.A. – the result of 'a visible stir, partly the rustle of a new hope, partly the stutter of a new despair'" (*1973, Bombay: Asia Publishing House*).

The most notable figure acknowledged as the first 'new poet' in Indian English literature to express a modern Indian sensibility is Nissim Ezekiel. His first book, *A Time to Change*, is considered a landmark. His appearance on the Indian English literary scene marked a new awakening – a new trend and a new attitude toward life and literature. The Writer's Workshop, too, emphasized the necessity of the private voice in poetry – concrete rather than abstract, precise and lucid in its statements.

Ezekiel's major themes include love, personal integration, modern urban life, and spiritual values. His poetry largely grows out of his own life and experiences. His first volume focuses on people, places, memories, and situations, carrying with them moments of literary reflection, revelation, and vision.

The opening poem of this volume, 'Double Horror,' engages with the corruption of the outer world, searching for its roots. *A Time to Change* serves as an exemplary moral allegory, incorporating the journey and quest motifs. Ezekiel's poetry operates on several levels: the sensual, the intellectual, and the spiritual. Additionally, two other key aspects of his work emerge – the confessional and devotional elements. Many of his poems blend confession, autobiography, and prayer. His portrayal of failures in love and sex often revolves around two types of failures: a frozen lack of commitment and dissatisfaction with the act itself. *A Time to Change* captures the journey of a man leaving his home, both physically and metaphorically, in search of meaning and change.

Like Kolhatkar, Chitre, and Pritish Nandy, Ezekiel is not an experimentalist, but his language possesses its own distinctiveness, similar to the style of R. K. Narayan. His poetry is lucid, rhythmically subtle, and scrupulously honest in its effort to be accurate, calm, and deliberate. Almost all the poems in his volumes explore a variety of themes such as love, sex, death, loneliness, and prayer. These poems testify to Ezekiel's consistent preoccupation with both the banality and complexity of modern civilization, as he perceived it in the Indian context.

Another notable figure among the 'new poets,' next to Ezekiel, is Dom Moraes, the son of the famous journalist Frank Moraes. Dom Moraes is one of the finest Indian poets writing in English, with strong affinities to the poetry of Wordsworth and the Romantics, sharing their mystical and visionary qualities. However, as an expatriate who had lived far from India for an extended period, Moraes adopts a somewhat Naipaul-like attitude toward his homeland, expressing a sense of non-belonging in his poetry.

Like Nissim Ezekiel, Moraes prefers English as his mother tongue. His first volume, *A Beginning*, won the Hawthornden Prize, and his second volume was recognized by the Poetry Book Society. His poetry is inevitably a product of his encounters with contemporary reality, as well as his subjective experiences. In his poem *Letter to My Mother*, Moraes expands the personal into the universal, capturing the emotional depth of the son-mother relationship.

P. Lal, a pioneer of the modernist movement in Indian poetry in English, founded the Writer's Workshop for new poets. Rejecting the romanticism and Victorianism of earlier poets, particularly Aurobindo, Lal was heavily influenced by T. S. Eliot's emphasis on natural voice, realism, and contemporary verse techniques. His poetry, with its economy and precision, is both evocative and suggestive. In this way, P. Lal serves as a bridge between the old and the new in Indian English poetry.

Another poet who, like Sarojini Naidu, shares some similarities with Lal is Mokashi Punekar. His poems often carry intellectual and moralistic dimensions. One of his significant contributions to Indian poetry in English is his translation of Kalidasa's *Ritusambaram*.

A major poet following Nissim Ezekiel among the new poets is A. K. Ramanujan. Though he is often considered a 'foreign poet' of native India, Ramanujan is deeply connected to his roots as a poet and translator. He translated Kannada and Tamil classics into English, bringing regional literary traditions to a wider audience. His most well-known work is *The Interior Landscape*. As a professor of Dravidian studies, his understanding of linguistic and metrical forms greatly influenced the style and structure of his poetry.

Ramanujan's deep knowledge of folklore also provided him with themes, ideas, images, and symbols that enriched his work. Coming from a South Indian Brahmin background, he often infused his poetry with a sense of nostalgia and sentimentality. Alienation, both personal and cultural, is a recurring theme in his poetry. He was a product of both modernization and Westernization, and his poetry reflects the tensions and changes within his identity.

In addition to themes of expatriation and alienation, Ramanujan often embraced a confessional dimension in his poetry. Much of his work centres around his personal experience, particularly the inner world of memories, and the continuous dialogue between past and present. His poetry explores the conflicts and tensions that arise between the self and the outer world.

At its core, Ramanujan's poetry is deeply subjective, drawn from memories and impressions of his familial past. His obsessions with his past and roots made him rely heavily on memory and poetic strategy. The memories of his family – his aunts, sisters, father, and mother – and his childhood in a traditional South Indian Brahmin household are central to his work.

As Ramanujan himself once said, creativity comes from sustained attention to one's own experiences, locality, and landscape.

As many critics have pointed out, Ramanujan's inner world encompasses not only memories but also fears and desires. These include his fear of snakes, sexual desire, the longing for unreflecting identity and harmony, and an anxiety that he perceives as part of a continuous process. To truly understand his poetry, one must engage in a careful study of his work. Some of his most significant poems include *Small Scale Reflection on a Great House, Some Indian Uses of History on a Rainy Day, Prayers to Lord Murugan, The Striders,* and *Love Poem for a Wife,* [1].

A key achievement of Ramanujan's poetry is the technical perfection, objectivity, and poise that mark his work. His poems are calm, measured, and elegant, yet rich with emotional depth.

William Walsh, commenting on the significance of Ramanujan's poetry, remarks: "His manner is limpid, calm and unaffected, natural in its run and tone and beautifully measured to its purpose. It has neither the agitation of his American context nor the foggy quality inseparable from British English, and it communicates with complete ease and Indian sensibility." (Ramamurthy, 1995, Macmillan, p. 48).

Ramanujan's poetry reflects his voluntary exile from India. His first collection, *The Striders* (1966), received wide recognition and includes many polished poems, both thematically and in terms of craftsmanship. Notable poems in this volume include *The Striders*, *Snakes*, *A Poem of Particulars*, and *An Image for Politics*. His use of vivid, suggestive imagery, combined with precise language, makes his verbal portraits remarkable. The linguistic precision in his work is matched by the depth of his emotional insight.

His second volume, *Relations* (1972), published by Oxford University Press, is an even more mature achievement. It serves as a bridge between childhood and age, as well as between India and America. Many of the poems in this volume explore the poet's memories of his relationships and the ambiguous sense of freedom that life away from his family affords him. Ramanujan's awareness of history is evident in both his first and second volumes, but in *Relations*, the power of his historical awareness is more strongly projected, particularly in the family-oriented poems.

He has a powerful sense of historical tragedy and individual suffering. The consciousness of India's tragedy and the experience of being Indian are deeply expressed in his poems such as *'Compensations'*, *'Conventions of Despair'*, *'Prayers to Lord Murugan'*, and *'The Last of the Princes'*.

To sum up, his poetry reflects the specific cultural context of India, and his true poetic greatness lies in his ability to translate these experiences into the terms of another culture. He skillfully uses the English idiom with unmatched precision. His command over imagery is extraordinary. As a meticulous artist, he always sought perfection before publishing any work.

Another poet who bears resemblance to A. K. Ramanujan is R. Parthasarathy. Both are expatriate writers from the South, and both share a preoccupation with their familial and cultural past. Their poetry is often personal, reflective, and confessional. Parthasarathy began his career with a strong faith in English, but after visiting England, he returned to India with a new understanding and began writing in Tamil. He has published just one collection in English, *'Rough Passage.'* (1977)

The poem's theme unfolds in three parts, with the theme of identity exploring two cultures. The first part, *'Exile'*, contrasts European culture with Indian culture. The second part, *'Trial'*, explores the testing of loyalties and celebrates love as a present and tangible reality. The third part, *'Home-coming'*, conveys the urgency of the self to return to where it truly belongs. The cycle completes itself, making *'Rough Passage'* a personal testament.

Finally, R. Parthasarathy greatly admired Ramanujan's poetry, particularly the way Ramanujan used his memories of growing up in a South Indian Brahmin family to recapture elements of Tamil culture. Like Ramanujan, Parthasarathy sought to bridge the gap between Indian English poetry and Tamil poetry.

After 1960, Indian poets began using the English language less formally, influenced by the colloquial English found in Western poetry. While they inherited the British literary tradition, poets like Shiv K. Kumar, Gieve Patel, Daruwalla, Adil Jussawalla, Jayanta Mahapatra, A. K. Mehrotra, Arun Kolhatkar, Dilip Chitre, and Keshav Malik made their poetry more engaging and distinctive. Along with Nissim Ezekiel, A. K. Ramanujan, and R. Parthasarathy, these poets liberated themselves from earlier tendencies toward generalized depictions of India, offering fresh perspectives.

In addition, women writers have held a unique place in Indian English literature both before and after independence. Their contributions, both thematic and literary, occupy a substantial position in the realms of fiction, poetry, and prose. The emergence of writers like Toru Dutt and Sarojini Naidu before independence marked the beginning of a new era of freedom and emancipation for Indian women.

Most of the women writers before independence focused on personal and autobiographical themes, whether in fiction or poetry. However, the post-independence era, with its focus on freedom and the feminist movement, led to a shift. Writers like Kamala Das, Gauri Deshpande, and Mamta Kalia wrote confessional poetry that reflected the influence of these movements. Their work was unconventional and modern, often challenging traditional values relating to love, marriage, home, and family. In their poetry, self-revelation seemed more like a form of defence against societal expectations.

Overall, modern Indian poetry in English has developed its own distinctive stance, setting it apart from earlier poetic traditions. Most of the poets wrote in English not out of external necessity, but as a form of inner compulsion. They found joy in expressing themselves in English, using the language as a medium to convey their native culture, Indian sensibility, and heritage. This modern poetry departed from older traditions such as Miltonic, Romantic, and Victorian forms, marking a significant evolution in the literary landscape.

In addition, these poets rejected older themes and forms, as well as the national classics and mythology, opting instead for fresh approaches to poetry. They sought perfection in the art of communication and presentation, emphasizing maturity, depth, clarity, and precision. By accepting English as one of the national languages of India, they elevated the language to a platform of international recognition, contributing to the growth of Commonwealth literature. The establishment of the Writer's Workshop in 1958 further exemplified their commitment to fostering a new, more contemporary literary tradition.

CHAPTER-2

A.K. Ramanujan's Creative Vision

A. K. Ramanujan is one of the three most significant Indian poets writing in English. The other two are Nissim Ezekiel and Kamala Das, just as Mulk Raj Anand, R. K. Narayan, and Raja Rao form the big three of Indian English novelists. A study of his poetry reveals a gradual evolution of his art and genius. As a genuine trilingual poet, he had much to offer, and he knew how to express it, both in English and in his native tongue. Therefore, his poetry carries an unmistakable authenticity in both tone and treatment.

His work is not easy to read, as it combines the vision of a folklorist, the insight of a poet, and the skill of a translator. He successfully turned the expatriate condition and post-colonial experience to his advantage, bringing the image of 'India' alive in his poetry. The purpose of this chapter is to evaluate A. K. Ramanujan as a postcolonial English poet, examining the development of his work and assessing his poetry.

Born in Mysore in 1929 into a well-to-do family, Ramanujan was both an expatriate and a postcolonial poet. His knowledge of three languages, early education at D. Bhanumaih's high school, and his Ph. D. in Linguistics from Indiana University in 1963 shaped his understanding of how to present India through poetry.

Ramanujan also had a personal history marked by significant experiences. He fell in love with a Keralite Syrian Christian woman, and ironically, the marriage ended in divorce. Similar to T. S. Eliot,

Ramanujan was drawn to Buddhism, and in 1963, he went to Sri Lanka with the intention of exploring this path. The influence of Buddhism remained with him throughout his life.

Afterward, he joined the University of Chicago as a professor and passed away in 1993. Before being recognized as a postcolonial poet, Ramanujan was known primarily as an Indian English poet, and more specifically, an expatriate Indian English poet. As a trilingual writer, translator, and folklorist, however, he successfully assimilated the cultures of his native India and the country of his migration, the United States.

Ramanujan made a multicultural commitment and transcended the limitations often associated with expatriate poets. B. K. Das aptly cites S. S. Dulai's critical observation on Ramanujan's poetry: "His poetry is born out of the dialectical interplay between his Indian and American experience on one hand, and that between his sense of his own self and all experience on the other; its substance is both Indian and Western." (Pande, S. N., 2001, Atlantic Publishers, p. 84)

To evaluate post-colonialism, it is essential to understand that it concerns national culture after the departure of imperial powers. However, in practice, it must be considered in reference to colonialism. Post-colonialism is a state of consciousness, much like colonialism itself, and colonialism encompasses both political and cultural imperialism.

Thus, myth and history, language and landscape, self and the other – these are all crucial elements of post-colonialism. According to postcolonial theory, one of the major themes in the literature of postcolonial countries is the resistance to the former colonizer. It is also assumed that writers who 'write back' to the centre represent the people of their societies authentically. A. K. Ramanujan is one such writer, whose poetry authentically represents indigenous traditions and native culture in artistic terms.

To elaborate, both A. K. Ramanujan and R. Parthasarthy drew strength for their English poetry from an indigenous literary tradition. This connection to their cultural roots provided a framework of reference and values in their work. In contrast, for Nissim Ezekiel, Indian-ness is more of a state of mind.

Ramanujan's five volumes – *The Striders* (1966), *Relations* (1971), *Selected Poems* (1976), *Second Sight* (1986), and *The Collected Poems of A. K. Ramanujan* (1995), which includes *The Black Hen* – bear testimony to his Indian-ness. While his poetic output is relatively modest, it has earned him recognition and established his poetic talent. Through his work, Ramanujan interpreted the soul of India to the Western world.

His greatness as a poet lies in his ability to poetically fuse the experiences of the 'outer' world with the responses of the 'inner' world. This fusion reflects his deep engagement with the Indian ethos, psyche, and its pure spirit. What is especially remarkable in his work is his precision in combining skeptical views of real life with his poetic expression.

The principal reason why critics, both in India and abroad, continue to write about Indian English poetry – and about Ramanujan in particular – is not only because he is historically significant in the study of post-Independence Indian English poetry but also because his work possesses a unique character. His respect for the craft of poetry has elevated his work beyond mere expressions of emotion or ideas, giving it a depth and resonance that continues to captivate readers and critics alike.

According to Adil Jussawalla, "A. K. Ramanujan is perhaps the first Indian poet who consistently shows Indian readers that craftsmanship is as important to a poem as its subject matter." (Abidi, S.Z.H., 1979, Prakash Book Depot, p. 285)

Furthermore, S.Z.H. Abidi notes that Ramanujan, as a poet, was deeply aware of the importance of craftsmanship in poetry, striving to produce examples of 'mellow magnificence' through the meticulous cultivation of poetic form. He also represented a poetic sensibility that was unique, placing him at the forefront of critical attention among major contemporary Indian English poets.

To study Ramanujan critically, one must recognize that he was already influenced by the best of modern Indian poets from the West before he began writing his own poetry. His interest in translating classics from Kannada and Tamil, coupled with his engagement with both old and new Indian literary traditions, undoubtedly shaped his creative sensibility.

Therefore, understanding the relationship between his original works and his translations is not straightforward. It is challenging to pinpoint exactly how one influenced the other. However, a critical examination of his poetry, starting with his first volume *The Striders* (1966), reveals that Ramanujan gave equal importance to both his original and translated works, viewing both as creative acts. Over time, his poetry demonstrated a distinctive sensibility – one that uniquely blends Indian and Western elements through the medium of English.

Ramanujan comments (R. Parthasarthy, 1976, Oxford University Press, p. 95-96): "English and my disciplines (linguistics, anthropology) give me my 'outer' forms – linguistic, metrical, and logical – and other such ways of shaping experience. And my first thirty years in India, my frequent visits and field trips, my personal and professional preoccupations with Kannada, Tamil, classics, and folklore give me my substance, my 'inner' forms – images and symbols. They are continuous with each other. I no longer can tell what comes from where."

The dual nature of Ramanujan's poetic sensibility is, therefore, widely accepted. Tuqi Ali Mirza, a critic, rightly observes that Ramanujan revealed himself not only as a great craftsman but also as a poet of substance. His work bears the marks of all great poetry, transforming the ephemeral into the permanent. His greatness as an artist lies in his detachment. R. Parthasarthy also offers an insightful observation, stating that Ramanujan's real greatness lies in his ability to translate his experiences into the terms of another culture. His poetry is the product of a specific culture, yet it transcends its origins. His poetic craftsmanship comes into play when he translates his experiences and handles the English idiom with consummate skill.

This skill allows him to elevate what might otherwise be a limited or insular experience into something with a universal resonance. His fastidiousness as an artist is evident in how he transforms familial and communal experiences into authentic, sensitive poetic language, giving them a naturalness that resonates with readers.

Indo-Anglian poetry has made a significant contribution to the development of poetry in India. It has successfully voiced the multifaceted experiences of the Indian people. In this regard, poets like Ramanujan have employed a variety of techniques to convey their vision of life, shaping the landscape of modern Indian poetry.

A major poet who contributed significantly to Indo-Anglian poetry is A. K. Ramanujan. His substantial contribution to the growth and development of Indo-English poetry is unique. Rooted in the native ethos and tradition, yet with the sensibility of an expatriate, Ramanujan wrote with a deep sense of commitment. Although he was not a prolific writer, he carved out a distinct place for himself by blending diverse themes and perspectives.

As S. N. Pande notes, Ramanujan's inherent genius enabled him to merge the critical, rational outlook of the West with the rich cultural and spiritual heritage of the East. Pande also affirms that Ramanujan's poems strongly reflect his deep connection to the East, even though he spent much of his life in the United States. Despite his long exposure to Western culture, Ramanujan never ceased to be an Indian – a quality that is both an asset and a liability for him as a poet.

Ramanujan's poetry also vividly reprints the various sights, sounds, and aspects of nature as he perceived them. He responded to these with a historical, philosophical, and mythical sensibility. His work embodies a fusion of his perception of the eternal world with his inner imaginative responses, lending extraordinary depth and meaning to his poems. As K. R. Rao (M. K. Naik, Ed., 1982, Madras: Macmillan) observes, this combination of the external world with the poet's internal world gives Ramanujan's poetry a unique and powerful resonance.

> **"When poet reflects on the world around him**
>
> **And registers his reaction to it in a wistful,**
>
> **Thoughtful and photographic manner,**
>
> **He writes reflective poetry. On the other hand**
>
> **If his (thoughts) are turned towards the internal**
>
> **World of memories and he is weighing**
>
> **The significance or in significance of his own life,**
>
> **He writes introspective poetry."**[5]

Thus, the reflections around A. K. Ramanujan and his thoughts on the internal world of memories represent two distinct dimensions, both of which are essential to his poetic essence. He writes as a reflective poet when engaging with the outer world, and his major concerns are nature, love, and human heritage. Conversely, he writes as an introspective poet when immersed in metaphysical contemplation, spiritual illumination, and visionary experiences.

While many individual poets may excel in portraying one of these worlds, Ramanujan's singularity lies in his ability to blend these two dimensions effectively. He communicates the thrill and ecstasy of human experience, as well as the heightened states of consciousness he explores in his work. A. K. Ramanujan's art is nearly flawless, with the only notable shortcoming being the limited volume of his poetic output.

Ramanujan authored five volumes of poetry. His two early collections, *The Striders* (1966) and *Relations* (1971), showcase his poetic genius remarkably. The themes of his poetry include the lives of Indian men and women, family dynamics, love, death, cultural harmony, and the complexities of life. His poems on subjects like insects, relatives, and the Hindu way of life are intricate, yet they are treated with remarkable clarity and precision.

Ramanujan's first anthology, *The Striders* (1966), established his poetic sensibility. It is a slim but elegant collection, featuring poems like 'Snakes,' 'Breaded Fish,' and 'A River.' These poems present precise, vivid images of the objects they describe. As with the other poems in the volume, the title poem *The Striders* clearly demonstrates that Ramanujan's poetry is image-oriented. As S. K. Desai observes, the poem exemplifies Ramanujan's characteristic imagist strategies. He is "primarily an imagist poet," and his work can be described as the 'poetry of seeing' or of perception. (Cit., p. 67)

Being image-oriented means that Ramanujan has an eye for the particular, the precise, and the concrete. The poet excels in the craftsmanship of language and imagery. The poem further demonstrates that he has a keen eye for the specific physiognomy of the insect and an insight into its characteristic qualities. It highlights his observant nature and his interest in animals such as the striders and snakes.

To compare a small insect to a prophet shows the poet's sense of humour at work. The striders – New England water bugs – are superficially described. The scene of the 'bubble-eyed' and 'weightless' insect on the 'ripple skin of a stream' depicts the supreme ease with which the striders balance themselves on the flowing water.

This means that just as Moses walked upon water, the insect treats the surface of the water as its natural element, moving across it lightly and without any sense of danger. The entire experience, while echoing Hindu philosophy and myth, is presented through a Western lens.

This sensibility and objectivity, as we see in his later works, becomes a lifelong passion for Ramanujan. The extreme detachment, concreteness, and precision that characterize *The Striders* extend to nearly all of his poetry throughout his lifetime. Thus, the poet succeeds in evoking spiritual concreteness through the image of an ordinary amphibian.

Looking at all the poems in *The Striders*, we find recurring themes such as individual identity, the self, and the world, the relationship between mind and body, the tension between the past and the present, and the idea of time as flux.

In almost all of his poems, the poet relies on memory, transforming the distant into the immediate through what K. Raghavendra Rao calls 'reverse romanticism.' In poems such as *A River*, *A Hindu to His Body*, and *Conventions of Despair*, memory plays a crucial role in linking the past and present, with both shaping and defining each other.

However, the role of memory in his second volume, *Relations*, does not work as effectively in poems that require a direct expression of personal feelings. To maintain a distance from the personal and the private, Ramanujan prefers poetic modes that are ironic and imagistic. In *Self-Portrait*, for example, he adopts an imagistic mode to emphasize the fluidity of the self, which 'resembles everyone but myself.' He also skilfully combines irony and imagery in poems like *Looking for a Cousin on a Swing* and *An Image for Politics*.

Ramanujan's fine sense of particulars recalls John Donne's work from the seventeenth century. In his love poem *Still Life*, he captures the intricacies of love, loss, and longing. The interaction between the poetic self and memory, which is first conceived in *The Striders*, becomes a central element in this poem. Though autobiographical, *Still Life* is a deeply personal work, in which Ramanujan recalls a childhood experience of being terribly frightened when he saw snakes drinking milk.

At the end of the poem, the poet overcomes his fear of snakes. The poem shifts from the rural Indian setting to an urban Western context, suggesting the need to confront both real and imagined fears. The image of the subjective self-walking through the woods without fear represents this transformation. Similarly, in his poem *Of Mothers, Among Other Things*, Ramanujan begins with the self-relating to the mother's 'twisted black bone tree' and ends with the image of the self-licking bark in the mouth after observing the sensible fingers picking up grains of rice from the 'kitchen floor.'

The Striders also features *A River*, a poem that reflectively draws attention to the river *Vaikai*, which flows through Madurai, an ancient city of Tamil culture. Ramanujan's artistic strength lies in his ability to combine the visual with the conceptual. The images he creates are primarily visual, but beneath these patterns, we can sense their deeper beauty and modern consciousness. Two extreme stages in the river's life reflect the poet's Indian sensibility: one stage, when the river is dry, and the other, when it is full and flowing.

Such vivid word-painting is possible only by a poet like A. K. Ramanujan, who has a keen eye for the smallest details of even the most ordinary phenomena. The poem's ironic tone becomes apparent when it shifts from a reflective level to an introspective one. By seamlessly blending these two perspectives, Ramanujan encourages his readers to actively engage in constructing the poem's essential meaning.

Breaded Fish is another poem in Ramanujan's first volume that is rich in pictorial imagery, evoking memories that horrify the poet. Language is skilfully used to express these memories in poetic terms. Here, past memories find their objective correlative in the present, deeply sinking into the poet's consciousness and giving rise to the present lyric. The poem describes a *breaded fish*, which is made into a breaded dish, and the poet is invited to eat it. However, the fish immediately triggers certain memories for the poet, making him unable to eat it, even though it is thrust into his mouth. Thus, the past reawakens in the poet's consciousness, shaping his reaction to the present moment.

The poem is autobiographical and blends memory with desire. The poet's use of the crystallized image of the breaded fish expresses a deep-rooted memory that has become embedded in the poet's self-consciousness. This poem also demonstrates Ramanujan's skill in intertwining the present with the past, the vague with the concrete. The image evokes a forgotten memory that resurfaces, influencing the poet's response in the present.

Looking for a Cousin on a Swing is another example of a family poem from Ramanujan's first volume. In this poem, the poet's consciousness is dominated by his familial relationships, which serve as the principal sources of his inspiration. Living in a distant country, he constantly remembers and yearns nostalgically for his homeland and the various members of his family.

The poem offers a luminous evocation of family life through the use of vivid and telling images. As R. Parthasarthy rightly points out, the family is one of the central metaphors in Ramanujan's work. In this poem, the poet enshrines the memory of a cousin who was his playmate during childhood. Although the poem seems impersonal, it is written in a nostalgic mood, reflecting the poet's yearning for the past and the family connections that shaped his early life.

The Hindu is a remarkable poem that sheds light on several aspects of A. K. Ramanujan's art. Dr. Raghukul Tilak rightly points out the two contending sides of Hinduism in the poem: one of non-involvement and the other of a superior sense of detachment. Kulshrestha also notes that the poem highlights the self-deception inherent in the stereotype of the Hindu by showing how outward calmness thinly disguises violent inner disturbances during moments of crisis. Ramanujan's Hindu-themed poems, such as *A Hindu to His Body*, *The Hindu: He Reads His Gita and Is Calm at All Events*, and *The Hindoo – The Only Risk*, all unravel a deep ironic stance. The use of *OO* instead of *U* in *Hindoo* is one such example of the irony.

Being a Hindu himself, and descending from an orthodox Brahmin family, Ramanujan is skeptical about the God-fearing attitude of Hindus, which often insulates them in selfishness. What he hints at is the dual nature of the self: one is real, hidden, and secretive, while the other is apparent, pretentious, tentative, and false. The gap between the real and the apparent self is explored in these poems, where the true self remains hidden behind the veil of religion. In these works, Ramanujan catalogues what it means for him to signify the body as a Hindu.

The Hindu: He Reads His Gita and Is Calm at All Events employs the Petrarchan sonnet form and serves as a superb example of irony. The sacred Hindu scripture, the *Gita*, teaches one to control the senses, to be more humane and compassionate, and to achieve inner calm. However, in the poem, the persona has read the *Gita*, yet he has lost the spirit of its wisdom, revealing the gap between intellectual knowledge and the lived experience of its teachings.

He, through these poems, tries to ascertain that half-knowledge will never make an individual wise, and that one must not follow the *Gita* by its letter, but by its essence and spirit. His dig at some Hindus is reiterated in *The Hindu: The Only Risk*. The Hindu, whose knowledge of the self and the world is incomplete, biased, and selfish, has been made the victim of his stimulated irony. As a Hindu, he is well-versed in the *Gita* and likely to retain his calm and heart's simple beat in the face of his neighbour's striptease or a friend's suicide.

Ramanujan's ironic mode achieves its height in *Prayers to Lord Murugan*, where Lord Murugan is considered the ancient Dravidian God of fertility, joy, youth, beauty, war, and love. He is represented as a six-faced God with twelve hands, writes S. N. Pande. Ramanujan laments the present mode of prayers and the loss of ancient ritualistic practices at the altar of Lord Murugan.

On the whole, the most striking example of Ramanujan's obsession with his Hindu heritage is found in his poem *Conventions of Despair*, in which there is a tension or conflict between the claims of Western culture and those of Ramanujan's Hindu heritage. The poem *Snakes* highlights his mother, who used to feed the snakes with milk, while the child poet would feel panicky at the sight.

Then there are the several Hindu poems he has written. A Hindu is supposed to remain calm in all situations, but in reality, he is never calm during a crisis, as shown in his poem entitled *The Hindu: Who Reads the Gita*. However, his Hindu poems attest to a mask (such as reading the Gita or not hurting an insect). Ramanujan's motto is well expressed in the following lines from the poem *Conventions of*

Despair: "I must seek and will find my particular hell only in my Hindu mind" (A. K. Ramanujan, 1966, Vol. I).

In the present poem, there is a clash between his Hindu orthodoxy and his equally strong awareness of modern values and ways of life, such as watching striptease or joining the supporters of the nuclear test ban treaty. It is clear from this poem that Ramanujan's intense awareness of his Hindu heritage does not lead to blind acceptance of Hindu orthodoxy, because he is equally aware of both the strengths and the weaknesses of his racial ethos. He certainly admires the Hindu vision of the unity of all life, and this admiration is evident in his poem *Christmas*. Here, he emphasizes the impossibility of discriminating between a leaf and a parrot, a branch and a root, or even a tree and a human being.

According to M. K. Naik, an eminent critic, A. K. Ramanujan's articulation of the Hindu ethos produced poetry of the periphery, as he fully exploited the opportunities provided by his Hindu heritage and the memory of his early life. In poems like *Conventions of Despair*, we find a curious uncertainty in his reaction to Hinduism. However, through his work, he demonstrates to his contemporaries the supreme importance of having roots and a glimpse of vitality.

As an Indian English poet, A. K. Ramanujan was a unique figure in integrating both Indian and Western imagery. Referring to *Prayers to Lord Murugan*, he emphasizes the significance of classical Tamil poetry forms, incorporating them into his English poems. He also preferred classical or typical Sangam poems, which are characterized by a well-defined, intricate form. Additionally, he favoured the sharpness of imagery found in these classical Tamil forms.

This use of language is fused with its modern Western counterpart in his English poetry, much like T. S. Eliot and Ezra Pound utilized in their works. Thus, in *Prayers to Lord Murugan*, Ramanujan explores the deep sense of loss in the modern world, as Lord Murugan has lost significance in a spiritually bankrupt society.

In this regard, T. S. Eliot employs similar images of spiritual bankruptcy in his poem *The Waste Land*. The sharpness of the imagery in Ramanujan's work also recalls Ezra Pound's poetry. To affirm this, one might recall Ezra Pound's words: "An image is more important than an idea. It is a vortex or cluster of fused ideas and is endowed with energy." (Pande, S. N., 2001, Atlantic Publishers, p. 12)

A. K. Ramanujan shows change as a perspective in his poem *History* and, as an adult, remembers his childhood. The poem takes the reader into the midst of an action, and history becomes a reality of the present. Similarly, *Small Scale Reflections on a Great House* brings history close to the present, and the house is a past, a memory, and a tradition that uses continuity in his work. He uses it within a specific genre, like poetry, or in its relation to others, such as folklore and language. His extension of the cultural past into the present is not only at the specific Indian level but also at the universal, and this lies in his uniqueness as a theorist and writer par excellence.

To elaborate on A. K. Ramanujan's development as a poet, one must read his three important poems: 1) *Self-Portrait*, 2) *Conventions of Despair*, and 3) *Still Another View of Grace*. The first and foremost poem in this volume is *Self-Portrait*, written in the early fifties. The poem addresses the question of his individual identity in an apparently innocent manner, centring on the poet's obsessive preoccupation with self-questioning. It is one of the most obscure poems by Ramanujan. In this poem, the poet cannot, perhaps, portray himself and his personality in definite terms. He finds in his personality traces of his ancestors and, more particularly, of his father.

Subsequently, *Conventions of Despair*, one of Ramanujan's longest early poems, was written in 1957 in Pune. A unique feature of this poem is its linking of familial experience with a historical sense, which runs through much of Ramanujan's poetry. It anticipates the major thematic and stylistic concerns seen in his well-known poems like *A Hindu to His Body*, *The Hindu: He Does Not Hurt a Fly or a Spider Either*, *The Hindu: He Reads His Gita and Is Calm at All Events*, *The Hindu: The Only Risk*, and *Second Sight*, among others.

The poem opens with a reference to the poet's awareness that he should be modern. However, his description of modernity is a depiction of a modern hell, much like that of the marginal man. The development of thought in the poem is smooth, and the rhythmic variations are skilfully managed.

Additionally, the three parts of this poem are very distinct. He begins in his usual ironic style, addressing the requirements of modernity. The second part of the poem describes the nature and beliefs of orthodox Hinduism, including the belief in the tortures a sinner must endure in hell after death. The final part of the poem contains only four lines, in which, according to Paul Verghese, the poet describes his reactions to both modernity and orthodox Hinduism. Verghese also notes that most of Ramanujan's poems express an Indian sensibility sharpened and conditioned by Western education, and this is most evident in *Conventions of Despair*. In this poem, "caught in the dilemma of modern educated India, [the poet] rejects both the modern and the Hindu conventions of despair in favour of archaic despair." (Paul Verghese, 1971, Bombay: Somaiya Publications, p. 41)

To examine Ramanujan's development as a poet, the last poem, *Still Another View of Grace*, plays a very important role. It was originally published under the title *A Poem on Logic*. The poem expresses the poet's feelings of passion and love for his wife, but the tension arises from the fact that the poet persona is a Brahmin, like Ramanujan, while his wife is a Syrian Christian, like Molly Daniel.

Both of them have different approaches to love, shaped by the cultural contrast between their two communities, though they belong to the same land. If one considers the poet's obvious preoccupation with motifs of ancestral heritage and memory, the tension becomes even more intensified.

However, Ramanujan's marriage to Molly Daniel and his interaction with his inner life reduce themselves to the state of a mere 'mask,' because the pull between them is so irresistible. In the poem, the poet simply gets 'burned and burned,' and all the 'Commandments' 'crumble' in his father's past, as rightly affirmed by P. K. J. Kurup while commenting on *Still Another View of Grace*.

Kurup also writes that the lover in the poem is well aware of his Indian Hindu sensibility, shaped by his upbringing in a strict orthodox Brahmin family. However, E. Narendra Lal points out that *Grace* denotes the love or favour shown by a Brahmin to a non-Brahmin woman, suggesting that the non-Brahmin woman receives something modern or new life. Such views, however, overlook the irony that firmly anchors us in this poem.

To sum up, the success of the first volume of his poems, entitled *The Striders* (1966), lies in the effective transmutation of personal experience into poetic terms through ironic distancing, the use of sensuous imagery, and other poetic devices. The second volume of his verses is entitled *Relations*, which was published in 1971. This volume exhibits his poetic genius remarkably. It centres on family and social concerns and also continues the tradition of the earlier volume. As R. Parthasarathy rightly pointed out, family is the central metaphor of Ramanujan's poetry.

All the poems included in this volume solely depend on memory preserved in time. The ironic mode presented in his poems helps the poet put the memorized experience in new perspectives. This is cited in his poems like *A River* and *History*. The fact is that he has a historical sense, which he exemplifies in poems like *Compensations* and *The Last of the Princesses*.

The best example of this historical sense is his fine poem *Small Scale Reflections on the Great House*. In this poem, the poet uses irony effectively to relate the self-centred world of this house – a symbol of India – to the outer world and shows the Great House as past, memory, and tradition that cannot be dispensed with.

A. K. Ramanujan's second volume, published by Oxford University, is a mature collection of recollected personal experiences and emotions. The prominent feature of this collection is *The Presence of the Past*, because the collective nostalgia of a whole people looks back, often with an attitude of love-hate, to the past, being simultaneously drawn towards and repelled by it. What gives artistic validity to this collection is Ramanujan's ironic stance in dramatizing familiar day-to-day activities.

The little ironies of life are comically observed by this 'memory' in the first volume of poems, entitled *The Striders*. Similarly, the second volume of poems reflects his private insights through memory, with a professional note, perhaps, to provide moments of great anguish and loss. Almost all the poems in his second volume recount events of the past, which not only dramatize their significance in relation to the present but also, by virtue of their meditative tones, invite deeper reflection.

The memory of the past renders the self a 'theatre' within which events are recalled and juxtaposed, revealing recurring patterns of historical and individual tragedy. Such a concern for the poetic self leads him to reflect on racial heritage and assess its strengths and weaknesses. To define this, he quotes a suitable passage at the beginning of this volume from his classical Tamil anthology: *"Like a hunted deer on the wide white salt land, a flayed hide turned inside out, one may run, escape, but living among relations binds the feet"* (Classical Tamil Anthology, 1ˢᵗ-3ʳᵈ Century A.D.).

Thus, the epigraph is an effective explanation in itself of the identity and preoccupation discernible in many of the poems in this volume. However, the motive of exploring the past leads the poet to reassemble his childhood self and rediscover its meaning.

Despite being rooted in Indian cultural tradition, Ramanujan's poetry can also be read as a form of English-language poetry with modern themes and forms. It achieves a rare blending of the ancient and the modern, the Indian and the Western idioms. As defined by T.S. Eliot, Ramanujan too has this continuity from tradition to modernity, a continuity between his poetry, translations, and scholarship. As a writer, he has not received the kind of recognition he deserves. However, critics generally view him more as a translator than as a major Indian English poet.

To appreciate him as a major Indian English poet, one can look at his well-crafted poem entitled *Obituary*. As the title suggests, the poem *Obituary* deals with death and is written in a tone of grief; yet, there is more humour and wit in it than sorrow. The theme of the poem is treated in a light-hearted manner, though the title itself is mournful.

In fact, the treatment of the father's death is more comic and ironical than pathetic and poignant. For instance, references to 'debts and daughters' and 'a bed-wetting grandson' are amusing. The image of the house leaning on a coconut tree is also comic. But the comedy does not end there. The dead father was described as the 'burning type,' and the fact that he 'burned properly' is very amusing. Even more so, the poet notes that the father's birth by caesarean section in a congested Brahmin locality and his death from heart failure in a fruit market are both too amusing.

And last but not least, when the poet says: "He left us a changed mother and more than one annual ritual." (A. K. Ramanujan, Vol. II, 1971).

It means that the poet, in a mock-ironic tone, talks about the legacy left behind by the poor father. But the essential concern of the poet is brought out in the poetic fusion of the personal and impersonal. A sense of universality is achieved in linking tradition and concern. By depicting the father's poverty and the mother's grief over the loss of her husband, the poet affirms his real love for the departed parents.

If *Obituary* is about the father, *Of Mothers, Among Other Things* is an impressive reflection on the mother at various stages of her life. It begins with her younger days, when she was like 'the silk and white petal.' However, this pleasant reflection does not continue for long. When he expresses the changed state of his mother, the poet is introspectively drawn into grief. He says that in her old age, there is no trace of the 'silk white petal,' but only, "her four still sensible fingers slowly flex to pick a grain of rice from the kitchen floor." (A. K. Ramanujan, 1971, Vol. II)

The use of the word 'still' indicates a sense of immobility and change that has come over her in her old age. But in the fusion of the reflective and the introspective, we discern the poet's capacity to overcome his mother's helplessness and admire her willpower and determination to overcome the handicap of old age.

His poem *Time to Stop* in *Relations* (1971) strictly opposes excessive visits to a museum and too much preoccupation with modern paintings, which dull the sensitive approach to life. This means his quest was to present the presence of the past. *The Last of the Princes* is another poem from the second volume of his poems, *Relations* (1971). The poem describes the decline and fall of the Mughal dynasty of emperors.

It exhibits his sharp and acute historical sensibility. The poem combines familial experience with historical consciousness. It is a poignant poem about the fall of the Mughal empire, shedding light on the poverty and suffering of the royal family as they fall on evil days.

The poem begins at the time when Aurangzeb died, and the Mughal Empire lost all its glory. Its slow decay and disintegration are compared to a patient suffering from tuberculosis, slowly heading to its final end. This is a poem written in an entirely detached manner. Pathos is naturally the atmosphere of this poem, which is written entirely in an objective style. It shows his genius for condensing his material and using the most appropriate diction, reinforcing the effect he aims to create.

Similarly, *History*, like *Looking for a Cousin on a Swing* from the first volume, reveals how childhood impressions are recalled years later. Here, the narrator is both an eyewitness and a reporter who narrates an incident that occurred on the day his great aunt died.

In *History*, the poet shows change as a perspective and, as an adult, remembers his childhood. The poem takes the reader into the midst of an action to understand the reality of the present, but *Small Scale Reflections on a Great House* brings history closer to the present. The house is the past, a memory, and a tradition. The continuity applies to the experience, which transforms through time exposure into an apparent pattern.

In poems like *History* and *Obituary*, memory is used to reflect the poet's consciousness of his poetic self in relation to familial tragedy in the Indian context. In contrast, poems like *Compensations* and *The Last of the Princes* project a consciousness of tragedy in India and the experience of being Indian, along with the ancient chaos of the country.

Overall, we agree with S. N. Pande that Ramanujan's poetry expresses a poetic sensibility in which Indian subjectivity merges with Western objectivity. His work embodies something uniquely 'Indian' in its stance and a sensibility that accepts the past without romanticizing it, while also mocking it, yet not disowning it.

Poems like *Love Poem for a Wife, I*, *Love Poem for a Wife, II*, and *Routine Day Sonnet*, all included in *Relations*, evoke the love-hate relationship between husband and wife. However, India and America – the two opposites – remain separate in *Still Another View of Grace*, and it is only rarely that the poet is able to reconcile the two.

They come together only in perfect poems like *Still Another View of Grace*, which asserts the power of passion and its ability to overcome one's religious beliefs and moral sensibilities.

In *Love Poem for a Wife, I* and *Love Poem for a Wife, II*, the poet illustrates the ambivalent nature of his own self, the self of his wife, and the relationship between these two selves. In *Poem I*, the poet subtly expresses irony about sharing childhoods in a child marriage, while in *Poem II*, he highlights the difference between himself and his wife, who always wears a 'changing Syrian face.'

To reflect the diverse dynamics of this relationship, A. K. Ramanujan also touches on other family members and social rituals and institutions. He employs similar strategies in other poems such as *Any Cow's Horn Can Do It*, *History*, *Obituary*, *Elements of Composition*, *Ecology*, *Death and the Good Citizen*, *Son to Father to Son*, *Drafts*, *Extended Family*, *Love Poem for a Wife and Her Trees*, and *Death in Search of a Comfortable Metaphor*, among others.

To present the 'objective correlative' of emotion, Ramanujan wrote two poems like *Love Poem for a Wife, I* and *Love Poem for a Wife, II.* The first is rooted in the desire to overcome the alienation that keeps them 'apart, at the end of years.'

The poem is cleverly constructed around a commonplace idea, as the poet tries to recall some of his wife's actions by recreating the past. It can be seen as a piece of satire on choosing a mate and later regretting the inability to share each other's past. The poet is clearly emphasizing the obvious. *Small Scale Reflections on a Great House* is also a memorable poem in which everything 'lost long ago' revives in the poet's memory.

The poet tells us how a family draws together its different members. The poem begins with an Eliotian touch: "Sometimes I think that nothing that ever comes into this house goes out" (A. K. Ramanujan, Vol. II, 1971). Here, *Great House* symbolizes the undivided joint Hindu family, and the adjective *great* seems to be used ironically, as there is nothing particularly 'great' about it. In this family structure, identities are lost, swallowed up in the great mass of the family. To my mind, this poem is a fine example of Indian English poetry, in which Ramanujan speaks of the joint Hindu family, which is rapidly breaking up. He describes our own situation, offering 'hints and guesses' about the decline of the joint Hindu family system. Thus, it is a poem about contemporary life that invites our participation. In this lies the true greatness of the poem.

To illustrate *Conventions of Despair*, it can be said that Ramanujan's motto is well expressed in the idea of seeking and finding the particular hell that exists only in his Hindu mind. In this poem, the poet presents a clash between his Hindu orthodoxy and his equally strong awareness of modern values and lifestyles, such as watching a strip tease, for instance.

It is clear from this poem that his intense awareness of his Hindu heritage does not lead to a blind acceptance of Hindu orthodoxy. Instead, he is equally aware of both the strengths and weaknesses of his cultural ethos. He certainly admires the Hindu vision of the unity of all life, and this admiration is evident in his poem entitled *Christmas*.

To conclude, one may agree with S. N. Pande, who states that it was Ramanujan's rootedness in his own culture and his connection to his family and people that provided him with emotional stability. This stability allowed him to engage with the outside world. The values of acceptance and accommodation helped him open his doors to other cultures. The secret of his success in the U. S. A. was never based on a Western, work-oriented mind-set, despite being an expatriate. Thus, fulfilment and focus on work are possible only when one's priorities are clear and straightforward.

Through active memory, Ramanujan engages in an on-going interaction between the past and the present. His portrayal of relationships with those who are deceased is not irrelevant; rather, the real events of the past emerge with new meanings for the present. To better understand the present, he seeks to memorialize the past by retrieving, reinterpreting, and rearranging memories.

As long as there is memory, there is neither fear nor a loss of connection. In this way, the poet's inner and outer worlds remain equally vivid and vital. Memory plays a crucial role in the poet's life, providing the impulse for work and progress. These methods allowed Ramanujan to view his life steadily, even in the United States. In his second volume, *Relations*, memory becomes an organizing principle, though it does not suggest a singular point of origin to which everything is linked.

A. K. Ramanujan's latest volume is *Second Sight*, published in 1986. In this collection, the poet addresses themes, attitudes, and tones similar to those in his earlier works. It is generally considered that the last poem in the volume reveals a profound sense of the poet's self. He asserts that the only sight he truly possesses is the first one – physical sight – and that sensory experience forms the foundation of all imaginative experiences. The modernist English influences of Ezra Pound and T.S. Eliot helped Ramanujan avoid the abstractions that characterized post-Independence Indian English verse.

In *Second Sight*, Ramanujan successfully blends forms and tropes derived from poets like W. B. Yeats and Wallace Stevens with the traditions of ancient Tamil and medieval Kannada poetry.

In *Pascal's Endless Queue*, there is a remark about A. K. Ramanujan: "You are Hindu, aren't you? You must have second sight." (A. K. Ramanujan, 1986, Vol.) To explore one's Hindu self, one must fumble and strike a light to regain both the first and only sight.

Similarly, in *Elements of Composition*, the poet reflects on the process of understanding the self, as well as the non-living elements and mechanical aspects of existence. His ever-growing sense of constant change leads him to perceive his existential self-more clearly. To fully understand the poet's stance at a certain stage in his quest for the self, one must recognize his integrity and the authentic existence of the self, which requires no external stimuli.

Only comprehensiveness can cope with the complexity of reality. It is only through this that someone, with a philosophic detachment modified by a cool, analytical, scientific spirit, can recognize others and compose the elements of a well-known list – father's seed and mother's egg, earth, air, fire, water, carbon, gold, magnesium, and so on. It is the sum total of everything he has seen, touched, and loved.

Thus, the poem is similar to *Self Portrait*, in which the identification of the self is presented through different attitudes and identities, each of them real in feeling and mysterious in apprehension. As he says in *Self Portrait*, "I resemble everyone but myself." This same trend is also evident in his poem *Drafts*, where he presents the view of the self as absurdly destined to assume an identity imposed by forces beyond one's control. A remarkable quote from *Drafts* reads: "The DNA leaves copies in me and mine of grandfather's uncle and programs of much older music; the epilepsies go to an uncle." (Ramanujan, A. K., Vol. III)

The variety of thematic concerns expressed by the poet about the modern man's search for identity is notably presented in *Extended Family*. In this poem, the poet reflects on his innate self and discovers its inertness and resemblance to others. He presents a self that is rooted in his native culture.

Hence, he nostalgically illustrates how he bathes like his grandfather, slaps soap on his back like his father, but dries himself with an unwashed towel. Like his mother, he listens to the morning songs, though they are faint and in Japanese.

In short, these poems offer valuable insight into the poetic self's concern with how the elements of self are formed and passed down, reflecting a typical traditional-modern sensibility at work.

If one wishes to assert the poetic self's oneness with all life through the exalted visualization of the body as the image of the soul, as seen in earlier poems like *A Hindu to His Body*, *Christmas*, and *A Poem on Particulars*, one must also look at his poem *Death and the Good Citizen*, which echoes the self's desperate craving for the preservation and perpetuation of life.

Towards the end of his creative career, A. K. Ramanujan seems to have been haunted by the images of his mother and father. The element of nostalgia takes him back to the days when he left for the United States. In a small but meaningful poem entitled *Farewell*, he echoes his fond memory of his mother.

He emotionally quotes, "Mother's farewell had no words, no tears, only a long look that moved on your body from top to toe." (Ramanujan, A. K., 1986, Vol. III). One also observes that Ramanujan's reflection on these images attempts to give an innate colour to his self by renewing himself and presenting the presence of the past. Like a child, the poet innocently tries to remember images such as "the bangles broken cutting across it," "unspoken dying through in the fruit market," and memories of his grandfather, father, and mother. In this way, he concludes his poems with a peculiar plight of the self that has to depend "on several / people / yet to come" for his future. Both his past and future are dependent on many others. This suggests that the self leaves its central position and, through a process of self-discovery, returns to the original position at the centre, acquiring wisdom in the process.

Here, self-discovery means recognizing the influences of external forms, while the nature of the self is romanticized, and the 'inner' self-encounters it. The end of everything in his poetry is his 'self,' which is not an enclosed entity, but rather a thing with real existence. Keeping in mind the freedom of the self to engage with points beyond itself – such as family, society, culture, religion, and the institution of marriage – without prejudice or bias, enables a smoothness and ease to proceed in the poet's exploration of identity.

Hence, his poetry remains distinctive and original, legitimizing its authenticity, originality, and cosmopolitan nature. In addition to this, a few notable poems include *Snakes and Ladders*, *Some People*, *Connect*, *Middle Age*, *Looking for the Centre*, *Looking and Finding*, *Dances in Hospital*, *The Watchers*, *Water Falls in Banks*, and *The Difference*, among others. Almost all the poems in this volume reflect the poet's insights and the 'second sight' of his self, exploring and reconsidering his Hindu heritage and poetic stance.

In poems like *Son to Father to Son*, the 'self' is ironically commented upon, as Ramanujan castigates both himself and the world around him. However, in poems such as *Middle Age, He Too Was a Light Sleeper Once, Looking for the Centre, Looking and Finding, Connect*, and *Dances in a Hospital*, he examines the image of the self, which reveals a sense of terror, righteous anger, and unfulfilled desire. In *Looking and Finding*, his search for humanity leads him to the terror he encounters in Assam and Punjab. In *Looking for the Centre*, the poetic self realizes that 'I am not at the centre' in the search for the centre of being. This same predicament is illustrated in *Connect*, where the poetic self is terrified by the dissolution around it.

His attitude toward God is expressed as a religious statement of a non-religious self in his poem *The Difference*. He presents the theme of obsession in three important poems from *Second Sight*. The first is *Extended Family*, the second is *Love Poem for a Wife and Her Trees*, and the third is *Looking for the Centre*. According to Niranjan Mohanty, it is rightly assumed that his poetry originates from the Hindu or Indian milieu.

It is also worth noting that the Hindu or Indian milieu constitutes the 'inner' substance of Ramanujan's poetry, while the Western milieu shapes the 'outer' substance. These two aspects always co-exist. To illustrate this co-existing nature in his poems, he exemplifies his work *Extended Family*.

In this poem, he compares family members and culture, recalling his grandfather and imagining his great-great-grandson. The poet's image of the naked self-bathing, as he rediscovers himself in relation to others, echoes his connection to his grandfather, bathing before the village crow. A. K. Ramanujan's effort to bring together the Chicago bulb and the Vedic sun symbolizes how America is to India what the poet is to his grandfather. His status as a member of an extended family, living simultaneously in different cultures and writing about them, is remarkably presented in *Extended Family.*

In *Looking for the Centre,* Ramanujan metaphorically states that physical reproduction occurs in the branches of 'family' 'trees,' with their roots in heaven and branches on earth. He also remarks that only eccentrics will look for the centre. In an anatomy book, one finds a map of heaven within the interior of the body.

Ramanujan's poetry closely examines the relationship between nature and the human body and explores the impact of culture and time on this relationship. The interaction between the body and the natural world is skilfully worked out in poems like *Love Poem for a Wife and Her Trees* and *Looking for the Centre.* The paradoxical nature of vision itself is revealed in poems like *Traces* and *Contraries.* In these poems, frames flow into each other, and the self is seen as a fluid field, not a fixed centre. Here, art and life interpenetrate, blurring their boundaries and dissolving their self-governance.

A. K. Ramanujan refers to the father's seed and mother's egg as contributing to his composition in his poem *Elements of Composition.* His portrayal of his father is tinged with sardonic sarcasm, while he describes his mother with love, admiration, and adoration. He explores his emotional relationship with his father in the poem *A Wobbly Top,* which is from his second volume. In this poem, both father and son are shown to have similar temperaments. In his poem *Extended Family,* a proverb, he recalls his father's habit of slapping soap on his back. He is also nostalgic about playing with his father at the age of five. Similarly, in *Son to Father to Son* from *Second Sight,* he remembers his sister, and in *Saturday,* he reflects on his brother and other members of his joint Hindu family. *Zoo Gardens Revisited* brings to mind memories of flamingos, black-faced monkeys, and long-legged aunts in white cottons. Thus, both the East and the West play a significant role in shaping his poetic vision.

To sum up, Ramanujan presents a unique representation of a typical Indian 'joint' family. As John Jones aptly points out, "It requires an ideal family, under the strong guidance of an ideal head, to live in peace and harmony under this system. Union is strength." (Pande, S. N., 2001, Atlantic Publications, p. 4)

In his poem *Death and the Good Citizen* from *Second Sight*, Ramanujan distinctly contrasts the conflicting nature of urban families and the extended or Hindu joint family. The sense of 'belonging,' which comes from living together for generations – a characteristic feature of the extended family – is absent in the urban family environment. The poet's respect for the extended family in Indian tradition, and his attempt to recover the sense of belonging, offers a cure for the rootlessness he feels. Thus, the recollections of Indian society bring tranquillity to those whose hearts connect with these alien veins.

In *On the Death of a Poem* from *Second Sight*, Ramanujan introduces a new element of terror, continuing art's encounter with the other. Similarly, in the poem *Drafts*, he reflects on the problematic relationship between the original and its copy, which resonates with the various drafts of a poem. On one hand, the mythical world of rituals is evoked, while on the other, the modern, realistic world is presented. In *He Too Was a Light Sleeper Once*, the poet does not resemble T.S. Eliot's modern man from *The Waste Land*, who feels "April is the cruelest month." Instead, the poet here was once a light sleeper, possessing a refined sensibility that allows him to respond to the subtle stimuli of life.

The Black Hen is a posthumous collection of poems. As an Indian poet, A. K. Ramanujan wrote his poetry not only in Kannada and Tamil, drawing on his knowledge of Indian folklore, myths, and classics, but also in English, conveying his experiences. His work is not limited to an Indian perspective; it is perceptible to readers worldwide – from Chicago in the West to Japan in the East.

Almost all of Ramanujan's experiences in Chicago extend beyond the boundaries of the Indian subcontinent. A fine example of his portrayal of these experiences is found in his posthumous collection *The Black Hen*. In this collection, he observes his experiences during visits to places like Chicago, Yukon, Japan, and China. During these visits, he examines human relationships, culture, and time, themes he had already explored in his earlier volumes.

According to Vinay Dharwadkar, A. K. Ramanujan was influenced by the thoughts of the Virashaiva tradition in Kannada, the Srivaishnava tradition in Tamil, Spinoza's philosophy, Zen Buddhism, as well as the philosophies of Pascal and Borges. Similarly, his conception of time was shaped by philosophical reflections, which deeply influenced his poetry.

Vinay Dharwadkar finally comments: "Ramanujan was involved in mapping the mutual interdependencies of body, nature, culture, and time until they cover an immense span of human and natural history." (A. K. Ramanujan, 1995, p. 27) The collected poems begin with the poet's thematic perspective, exploring this theory. In the second part, he critically engages with his poems, and in the final section, he hypothetically concludes the structure of the poem.

Almost all the poems in this posthumous collection reflect his effort to balance between two worlds: the world in which he was born, and the world he came to know. Several notable poems appear in this collection, including: 1) *The Black Hen*, 2) *Foundlings of the Yukon*, 3) *Shadows*, 4) *At Zero*, and 5) *Salamanders*.

The Black Hen is the final volume of Ramanujan's poetry, published posthumously. He was always in favor of natural poetry, believing that if poetry did not come as naturally as leaves grow on a tree, then it was better not to write it at all. *The Black Hen* represents rural life and offers a picturesque description of the hen that both scares the reader and evokes memories of the poet's grandmother's time.

The poem contrasts the voices of silence and sound by juxtaposing the past and the present, the urban and the rural, the aesthetic and the artificial. This contrast brings out the sense of the 'otherness' and terror in the creative process. The fixed gaze of the black hen's red round eyes, directed at the poet, captures this unsettling sense, making the poet himself feel frightened.

As a folklorist and Sanskrit parable writer, Ramanujan illustrates the story of the foolishness of four egoistic Brahmins who travelled abroad to study all the sixty-four arts. Though they were well-versed in the Shastras, they lacked practical common sense. In an attempt to demonstrate their knowledge, they tried to bring a dead tiger back to life. However, in the process, all but one of them lost their lives. The fifth Brahmin, who had common sense, was saved. This parable serves as a metaphor for the gap between theoretical knowledge and practical wisdom.

To exemplify great Indian legends, A. K. Ramanujan wrote a compelling poem, *Traces*. In this poem, he presents remote stars, 'light years away,' belonging to a different galaxy and time. These stars are humanized as 'the seven / sages and the Milky Way.' For Indians, the Sapta Rishi (Seven Sages) and the Milky Way are intimately connected with life, as one reads the stars to gain insight. Thus, *Traces* asserts that art is based on humanization, but in a limited way.

Ramanujan's second poem, *Foundlings of the Yukon*, from *The Black Hen*, is about the accidental discovery of seeds by miners in one of the coldest regions of the earth. The poem takes us across continents and subcontinents. The Yukon Valley, temporally and spatially distant, is at the farthest corner of the map. The civilization buried by a landslide is not dead. It is alive, revived by the seeds buried long ago, which sprouted within forty-eight hours of being planted. In this way, the poem links time, continents, nature, literature, and literary movement.

In *Salamanders*, Ramanujan explores the relationship between man and salamanders. He illustrates how salamanders are born in the slashes of the woods after the rain but eat fire. Similarly, in *At Zero*, he speaks of how at 'zero hour' there is a universal standstill. To illustrate this, he uses the image of Brahmin widowhood. The stillness, in this case, represents blankness, which is compared to the blankness of a Brahmin widow forced to live a plain life without the colour or vibrancy of traditional dress.

Not Knowing is a recent poem included in *The Black Hen*. In this poem, Ramanujan intensifies the self-definition and self-search, exploring these themes with painful depth.

Similar to this, his poem *Trilogy* deals with a common theme: the mystery of poetic creation. The poet links man with nature in his poem *One More on a Deathless Theme*. Here, Death traces man's relationship with flora and fauna. He introduces the concept of *Ardhanarishvara* from Hindu mythology, where Lord Shiva accepts 'Ardhanari,' recognizing that one half is a woman.

In his poem *Fog*, Ramanujan reflects on the transition from rural to urban scenes. However, his remarkable use of two images tied to the annual calendar in *August* highlights his greatness as a poet. In it, he compares the strong feeling of the passing months to the coffee made by his grandmother, evoking a vivid sense of nostalgia. Similarly, the heat of April in June is compared to the persistence of prayer, capturing the intensity of both.

In *On Not Learning from Animals*, he starts with a positive note, emphasizing the need to learn from animals. He praises their honesty, contrasting them with humans, who, he suggests, are often hypocritical.

As a poet, Ramanujan not only wrote about Hindu heritage and the cultural past of India but also explored mythological stories. In *Mythologies, I*, he revisits the Krishna and Putana. In this story, the divine child Krishna not only sucked away the poisonous milk but also took Putana's life, redeeming her from her curse.

In *Mythologies II*, Ramanujan explores the Hindu myth of Lord Vishnu's incarnation as Narasimha, the half-man, half-lion form. Narasimha kills the demon king Hiranyakashipu, who is the atheist father of Prahlada, a devout follower of Lord Vishnu. This myth is central to Ramanujan's portrayal of divine justice. In *Mythologies III*, the poet explores the Hindu concept of sexual union between a lawful husband and wife, which is seen as a union with the divine. The poet juxtaposes the spiritual devotion of one individual with the physical love between two others, subtly commenting on the superiority of the spiritual over the physical or material realm.

Ramanujan's deep knowledge of Indian myths and folklore is evident in these works, which blend cultural heritage with poetic expression. This aspect of his poetry is still respected in post-colonial literature. However, Ramanujan's work also reflects his scientific sensibility, such as in his poem *Pain: Trying to Find a Metaphor*. Here, he uses the concepts of acid rain and the Bonsai tree – two foreign elements, one scientific and the other cultural – to construct metaphors. Acid rain, which has been a problem in North American cities, and the Bonsai tree, a Japanese art form where trees are kept small and stunted, serve as metaphors for human pain, both suggesting unnatural conditions that inhibit growth.

In *Bosnia* and *A Report*, Ramanujan takes a more global perspective. *Bosnia* reflects on the atrocities committed in Bosnia, Biafra, and Bangladesh during their respective wars, offering a stark portrayal of human suffering. *A Report*, on the other hand, lists historical figures – Hitler, Stalin, Lenin, Gandhi, and others – who created history, yet are ultimately rendered irrelevant in the face of on-going human conflict and decay. The poem thus takes a broad, global view of history, showing how great figures and their actions fade against the backdrop of global suffering.

The final poem of Ramanujan's last anthology, *Fear No Fall*, is a devotional piece that tells the legend of the Tamil saint Arunagiri. In a vision, Arunagiri is inspired to sing of the god Murugan by an old man who gives him his first line of verse. The poem captures Arunagiri's spiritual transformation, moving from doubt to the divine through the act of song, symbolizing the poet's own connection to the sacred.

To conclude, throughout his work, A. K. Ramanujan traverses both the ancient cultures, like the myths of the Yukon Valley, and the contemporary issues of modern life. His poetry reflects the intersection of old and new, the sacred and the secular, the personal and the global.

He has written the following important translations, faithful in spirit to his originals, in the tradition of spiritual love and from a classical Tamil context: *Speaking of Siva, The Interior Landscape, Poems of Love and War, The Hymns for the Drowning, A Guide to Lord Murugan*, and *Fifteen Tamil Poems*, etc.

It is possible to analyse the concept of religion in India through the central framework provided by his religious poetry. Ramanujan's translations of Bhakti poetry emphasize that the only route to salvation is total surrender to God. This concept seems to have influenced him tremendously in his later years.

The last poem of his final anthology is titled *Fear No Fall*. It transformed him from a spiritual seeker into a saint, allowing him to sing a devotional song. Thus, the poet's spiritual dilemma seems to dissolve as he embraces the choice of his works.

He chose to translate two important volumes of devotional poetry: one in honour of Siva, called *Speaking to Siva*, and the other in praise of Vishnu, titled *Hymns for the Drowning*.

Medieval saints wrote *Speaking of Siva* in Kannada in the 12th century, encompassing argument, song, debate, prayer, and narrative. It describes the different stages on the path to realization. This work was translated into English by A. K. Ramanujan as Bhakti poems. First published in 1973, it was reprinted in 1979. The collection contains the *Vacanas* of four Kannada medieval Shaivite saints from the 10th to the 12th century.

As introduced by Ramanujan in his preface, a *Vacana* is "a religious lyric in Kannada free verse." The word *Vacana* literally means 'saying' or 'thing said.' It represents the period of figures such as Basavanna, Devara, Dasimayya, Mahadevigakka, Allama Prabhu, and others.

The *Vacanas* are Bhakti poems primarily addressed to Lord Siva. These poems stand in opposition to the formal structures of classical Hindu texts. They challenge the great traditions of the Vedas, Vedic rituals, caste hierarchy, pan-Indian deities, as well as the local traditions of the *Puranas*, sacrificial rites, and religious deities.

To the Bhakti poet, true religion is the religion of the soul, and the spontaneity of worship is the hallmark of Bhakti. The Bhakti poet is a visionary, a mystic of the highest order, who reveals his own self-realization so that others may transcend the limits of their finite selves and attain a state of spiritual bliss.

Ramanujan presents several metaphorical terms that reflect his religious concept of devotion. According to S. N. Pande, the true experience of God, what the poet calls *krupa* (grace), cannot be expressed or recalled in ordinary terms. The *Vacanas* distinguish between *Anubhava* (experience) and *Anubhava* (the experience). Hence, the search for an unmediated vision through experience is unpredictable. In Bhakti poetry, or the poetry of mystics, mysticism is not merely a metaphor; it is a felt experience. The self-experience becomes a foretaste of immortality, transcending the mere level of intellectual or cognitive perception. Therefore, felt experience and creative expression must be fused.

On the whole, although Ramanujan was an expatriate Indian poet, he was deeply concerned with his Indian past, which spoke of an intellect and soul that were inextricably bound to and sustained by a tradition that was enriching and fulfilling.

It can always be affirmed that his *Speaking of Siva*, a translation of the Kannada *Vacanas*, provides the best solution to many of the gripping dilemmas of the modern man.

In his introduction to *Hymns for the Drowning: Poems for Vishnu*, Nummular discusses Ramanujan's method of translation:

"To translate is to 'carry across': metaphor'

Has the same root meaning. Translations are

Transpositions; and some elements of the

Original cannot be transposed at all.

For instance, one can mimic levels of diction,

Even the word plays, but not the actual

Sound of the words."[21]

By and large, one must say that A. K. Ramanujan's comment on the word *translate* is simply the Latin equivalent of the Greek word *metaphor*. In his essay *Classics Lost and Found*, Ramanujan notes that both words mean to 'carry across,' as aptly stated by S.N. Pande in his note on A. K. Ramanujan. When Ramanujan discusses *The Interior Landscape: Love Poems* from a classical Tamil anthology, he explains that translation is, in essence, the act of translating not just a poem into a foreign language, but also of translating a foreign reader into a native one.

He argues that there are two main themes in his *Cankam* poetry. The poems of *Akam* (the 'inner' part), which are love poems, and the poems of *Puram* (the 'outer' part), which address matters of good and evil, action, community, and kingdoms, among other things.

Thus, *Akam* poetry deals with the inner world, while *Puram* poetry explores the outer world. To understand the role of religion in his poetry, it is essential to recognize where his origins lie. A. K. Ramanujan, born into an orthodox South Indian Brahmin Hindu family, is often difficult to categorize as simply critical of Hinduism due to his ironic stance. He was a creative artist who could afford to remain silent on certain aspects of religion, particularly those associated with his Hindu upbringing.

His sense of ease in objectively viewing the world outside the self, his detachment, and his ability to amalgamate both the 'outer' and 'inner' forms make him a notable poet of true Indian consciousness. Hence, his ironic mode, sharp attitude, and sophisticated approach made him a rare figure in Indian poetry in English.

His use of myths, legends, and tales from epics, mostly Indian, remarkably presents us with the rich cultural heritage of his native land to ascertain their contemporary relevance. Myths remain central to a culture in spite of material progress and scientific invention. He was always in search of a link between the past and the present by invoking myths in his poetry. The poet always discovers the continuity of his own self in myth, and such use of myths makes him aware of the natural reality in the present.

In the case of Ramanujan, however, the myths often act as a background to sharpen the edges of his irony. He begins his poem *A Minor Sacrifice* with a familiar tale from the epic and follows it with an incident chosen from day-to-day life. Both tales in the narrative are conclusive and independent of each other.

S. N. Pande has rightly pointed out that Ramanujan established a connection, harping on the perpetual tension between the scientific temper and the God-fearing karma-adhering attitude. The above poem remarkably presents Buddhist and Hindu influences on A. K. Ramanujan. It does not resolve the tension, but the manner in which the poem ends suggests that killing or sacrificing insects or animals is an act of reproachful sin.

A. K. Ramanujan has written three important mythological poems: 1) *Mythologies, I*, 2) *Mythologies, II*, and 3) *Mythologies, III*. These poems are slightly different from *A Minor Sacrifice* in terms of the use of irony in degrees. The first poem of the mythological concern is *Mythologies, I*, which characterizes different mythological characters such as Krishna, Putna, Kansa, etc. In this poem, these characters evoke the myth.

To characterize these characters in this poem, his basic purpose is to show that being killed by God leads to the realization of salvation. The demon, like Putna, purges all her demonic qualities after her death.

To infuse all the poison into the poet's self, the poet prays significantly. Hence, he expects salvation to begin a new life with resurrection, depicted in a correct and precise manner.

To affirm this, the poet remarks: "The child took her breast in his mouth and sucked it right out of her chest. Her carcass stretched from north to south. She changed, undone by grace, from deadly mother to happy demon, found life in death." (Pande, S. N., 2001, Atlantic Publishers, p. 54)

To invoke the myth of Lord Vishnu, the poet exemplifies his second important poem, *Mythologies II*. To characterize the significance of these characters, he presents the figure of the tyrannical king, Hiranya Kashyapu, the atheist father of Prahlad, a devotee of Lord Vishnu. To prove his omnipresence and protect his devotee, Lord Vishnu appears from the concrete pillar of the palace in the form of a half-man, half-lion, and tears the king apart. This demonstrates how the poet's prayer enables him to present the myth with genuine faith in his Hindu roots.

In the third poem, *Mythologies III*, the poet critically analyses the relationship between a wife and her husband. In this poem, the poet dramatizes the faith of a wife who attempts to keep her husband away from her while she worships Shiva, according to a myth. However, the husband's selfish nature prevents him from understanding the meaning of 'OM, OM' and devotion.

To illustrate this, one is reminded of the poem *Chitra*, in which Rabindranath Tagore dramatizes the concept of 'Yoga and Bhoga'. The poet suggests that one is for the devotional spirit, and the other is for the body or the physical. In this juxtaposition, the poet exemplifies the superiority of the former over the latter.

Ramanujan's poetry, therefore, exemplifies a new perspective in which both the self at the centre and the self that returns are of equal importance because of the symbolic relationship that exists between them – one that permeates and animates them, as rightly affirmed by S. N. Pande in his notes on A. K. Ramanujan. In his volume *Second Sight*, Ramanujan successfully fuses the forms and tropes derived from poets like William Carlos Williams, Wallace Stevens, and W. B. Yeats, with the traditions of ancient Tamil and medieval Kannada poetry.

To conclude, one may argue that the themes and concerns of all the poems in *Second Sight* are consistent with those in his earlier volumes. Most of the poems in this collection are free from the preoccupation with motifs of ancestral heritage and memory.

A study of his poetry reveals that the central concern of many of his poems is a search for self-definition and stability, in which memory – reaching back to past generations – plays a vital role. In this light, all his poems delve deeper into the layers of Hinduism, the world, and the self. In poems about his family's past, the poet reflects on his childhood self and rediscovers meaning in an effort to identify, locate, and define the self.

Finally, to categorize him as a postcolonial poet, A. K. Ramanujan recreates characters in their own situations and brings the native culture to life in the English language. Hence, in his poem *Second Sight*, he asserts that the only sight he truly possesses is the first one – the physical sight. The sensory experience, indeed, forms the foundation of all imaginative experiences. Several poems in *The Striders*, *Relations*, and *Second Sight* reflect on the duality of art and life. This duality of art and life requires great craftsmanship, which was innately present in A. K. Ramanujan.

CHAPTER-3

A.K. Ramanujan's Critical Idiom

Appreciation is a complex activity in which all the powers of the mind work together toward one end. At the same time, to express those experiences, the poet's words have a lively awareness of all its virtues. A student can express the poet's experiences only when he understands the full meaning of the words, and this can be done by cultivating the faculty of poetic appreciation.

To cultivate this, no better approach can be proposed than daily exercise in sympathetic engagement with great poetry. Thus, we learn to appreciate through appreciation and enjoy through enjoyment, where the ends and the means are the same. To write an appreciation of a poem, it is essential for the reader to strip himself of personal prejudices and attempt to see something of the poet's vision. The poet appeals directly to the poet within us, and our real enjoyment of the poetry depends on our own keenness of imaginative apprehension and emotional response. When we understand something of the poet's viewpoint, we then ask ourselves what it is that we like.

The next question should be whether the poet is able to present his experience convincingly, so as to grasp the total meaning and discuss the major themes and their development. This analysis of themes should go hand in hand with an examination of technique.

How does the overall grammatical structure of the poem express its meaning? What is the effect of the arrangement of the lines? How does the poet manage rhyme and rhythm? Is a traditional form being used, such as the sonnet or blank verse? If so, how is it related to the history of poetic usage in those forms? What types of images are being employed, and how are they arranged? How are the ideas developed? What is the poet's tone or voice? How do the words build up the complex impression we receive on a first reading of the poem? Finally, what has been achieved? Are there any weaknesses in the poem? Is the pleasure reduced by any lapses in technique? If we compare the poem to others of a similar kind, to what degree of excellence does it reach?

These questions are only pointers, and much depends on the reader's interpretation and understanding.

After a careful reading of the poem, we should be in a position to give its general meaning and to say something about the intentions of the poet or writer. This means there are two types of meanings:

1. **General Meaning**: This should be expressed simply in one or, at most, two sentences. It should be based on a reading of the whole poem. Very often, but not always, a poem's title will give you some indication of its general meaning.
2. **Detailed Meaning**: This should be given stanza by stanza, but without paraphrasing the poem or focusing on the meaning of individual words.

The detailed meaning may be written as a continuous paragraph, but care should be taken to express it accurately in simple sentences. Similarly, pay special attention to prose style and avoid expressing yourself clumsily or writing a list of sentences, each beginning with "In the first stanza," "In the second stanza," etc. You should show how the poet begins, how he develops his theme, and how he concludes it. If a poem is not divided into stanzas, make a rough attempt in your reading to divide the lines into fairly self-contained groups.

Every poem conveys an experience and attempts to arouse certain feelings in the reader. When one reads a poem and gives its general and detailed meaning, one should also try to decide what feeling the poet is attempting to awaken in the reader. A poem may affect different people in a variety of ways, and it is often impossible to define the poet's true intention. It is, however, most important to explain what one understands the poet's purpose to be, just as it is. But it is difficult to know the meaning of a poem and to appreciate it without reading it carefully.

Every poem is unique and has special qualities of its own. To appreciate a poem critically, it is necessary to learn how to recognize its 'special qualities,' also called devices, which can be found by analysing a poem. For the sake of convenience, devices may be divided into three groups: structural, sense, and sound. To write an appreciation of a poem, it is not enough to simply point out the devices. The effects they have and how they help the poet fulfil his intentions also need to be explained.

One may have to consider the following points to appreciate the thematic structure of a poem: 1) The significance of the title of the poem, 2) The poet's specialty and literary contribution, 3) The poet's point of view, 4) A brief summary of the poem, 5) The meanings of difficult words, phrases, usages, figures of speech, and devices, 6) A detailed explanation or meaning of each stanza, 7) The central idea or core theme of the poem, and 8) The poet's and the reader's conclusion.

Indian poets like A. K. Ramanujan developed a kind of mannerism in spoken form, and the post-1960 Indian poets in English tried to approximate this speech rhythm in their poetry. These poets followed this trend and attempted to recreate a just and lively presentation of Indian characters and situations in their poetry. The purpose behind employing such a technique was to capture the spirit of the personages in their actual form so that they could achieve the reader's total participation. This technique also aimed at creating a new Indian English idiom. Hence, Nissim Ezekiel was the first poet who undertook such a task.

The poetry of the moderns always serves a critical function, but to place them in the world of poetry, they possess a number of merits, one of which is 'modernity.' S. C. Harrex rightly points out that the new poetry is "a cultivated reaction against Indian romanticism and mysticism," and he describes *Savitri* as "a boring, spiritually obese non-poem" (Opt. Cit., K. S. Ramamurti, Macmillan Publications, P. 73). However, Bruce King goes to the extent of making a rather audacious statement, suggesting that Indian poetry in English begins only with Nissim Ezekiel, Dom Moraes, and A. K. Ramanujan, as noted in his recent book *Three Poets* (O.U.P.) and in *Modern Indian Poetry in English.*

Only A. K. Ramanujan and R. Parthasarathy were attempting to come to terms with their past on one level, while Aurobindo and Tagore were doing so on another, certainly much higher, level. By and large, the former's search was for identity at a historical, socio-cultural level, whereas the latter's search operated on a spiritual plane. The latter's search was grounded in the true Indian tradition, in which the emphasis was always on the conquest of the self and the realization of the self, rather than on the assertion of individual will or ego.

In the words of T.S. Eliot, two essential determining factors of modernity are variety and complexity. In modern poetry, the emphasis is perhaps more on complexity. This complexity is not merely sought in the subject matter itself; it is deliberately created in the treatment of a poetic experience, primarily through irony and paradox.

Like Nissim Ezekiel, A. K. Ramanujan too followed the same trend in his poetry. In this chapter, an attempt has been made to understand various aspects of him as a poet, poet-critic, and his poetry in general.

One may always affirm, in light of these considerations, that his poetry imbibes influences from diverse sources, i.e., intellectual, philosophical, and psychological. It is for these reasons that his poetry in English has been critically studied. The important aspects of his poetry are as follows.

R. Parthasarathy rightly points out that the family is one of the central metaphors in Ramanujan's poetry, through which he thinks. His poetry is full of references to his father, mother, wife, sister, aunts, cousins, nephews, and so on. Equally important in his poetry is his emphasis on his Hindu heritage. He has deep roots in Hinduism, which is an ancient religion, and he cannot escape his strong awareness of this heritage. Although his modernity was influenced by American culture, it has made him equally aware of the flaws and faults within his ancient religion.

The chief flaw he identifies is the superstition, such as the belief in hell and the tortures of hell, which dominate the Hindu mind. Hence, there is a tension in his mind, which is creative and results in some of the best poems he has written. To justify this, Sivaramkrishnan rightly points out that Ramanujan's poetry derives its depth and complexity from the mingling of Western modernity and Hindu orthodoxy in his mind.

Ramanujan's poetry, in this context, is essentially modern. It displays a wide range and complexity of thought and feeling. As a scholar, he reads widely, writes extensively, and translates meticulously. The principal aim of this chapter is to provide substantial help in studying his prolific work. His poetry includes echoes and allusions from a wide array of knowledge sources, ranging from philosophy and psychology to science and linguistics. It has often been observed that in Ramanujan's poetry, the image often leads the idea. In this respect, he has sometimes been contrasted with Nissim Ezekiel, in whose work the idea often eludes the image.

According to R. Parthasarathy, in Ramanujan, Mehrotra, Kolhatkar, and S.K. Kumar, the image is not only the springboard of poetic composition but also its kernel. "The Striders," a short poem from his first anthology, reveals a scientific precision in building up the image of the water bug sitting with extreme felicity on the surface of a stream. His extensive use of images in this much-discussed poem brings the life of the water bug before us with the picture of "the bubble-eyed water-bugs" perching "weightless" on "the ripple skin of a stream." This image is realistically portrayed in the poem. It even evokes a spiritual dimension and reminds us of one of Arun Kolhatkar's poems, "The Butterfly," where the butterfly has no future.

Ramanujan's poem "Snakes" often reminds one of D.H. Lawrence's poem of the same title, notable for its life-like imagery. To present the clash of Hindu orthodoxy and Western modernity, Ramanujan illustrates numerous such moments in his poems. The opening line of "Conventions of Despair" shows his strong awareness of and engagement with modernity.

The poem begins with a reference to the poet's awareness that he should be modern. He condemns modernity, describing it as hell, where the poet would be treated as a "Marginal Man." He also affirms that to be modern, a man should marry again, go to the movies, engage in scientific research, support the nuclear test ban treaty, and settle down in a foreign country. To comment on this, Paul Vergheese rightly points out (1971, Bombay: Somaiya Publications)

"The poems of A. K. Ramanujan express

An Indian Sensibility sharpened and conditioned

By a western education and it is most

Evident in 'Conventions of Despair' In

Which the poet caught in the dilemma of

A modern educated India rejects both

The modern and the Hindu conventions

Of despair in favour of an archaic despair"[2]

Like *The Striders*, *Self-portrait* is another modern poem, remarkable for its complexity, achieved through paradoxes.

According to Kirpal Singh, "'Self-portrait' is a beautiful imagist poem in which the poet reveals his predicament, i.e., everyman's predicament, as to what constitutes one's self" (1999, Cited, Vrinda Publications, P. 25). This poem not only illustrates a concern with the 'self' but also provides the framework within which a discussion of the 'self' in his poetry becomes relevant. In the words of Vinay Dharwadkar, "The self is more absence than presence in both private and public space" (P. 80, 1994).

Similarly, R. Parthasarathy's Rough Passage is, in a way, a search for self, where the poet attempts to initiate a dialogue between himself and his Tamil past. In contrast, Nissim Ezekiel seeks to dive deep into his own psyche. As he puts it in a poem called What Frightens Me, he has seen both the mask and the secret behind the mask.

Similarly, Kamala Das seeks to obtain an identity that is lovable in the ever-changing world and elusive realities of life. Thus, such complexity is discernible in poems like Conventions of Despair, Museum, and many others. However, Ramanujan speaks of an uncertain self, alien to its own viewer, in Self-Portrait, much like Nissim Ezekiel does in his poem Background, Casually, where he prefers to call himself a "poet-rascal clown."

To define modernism, Ramanujan's poem A River does not offer a traditional song of praise for the river; instead, he narrates the villagers' real experience. As a poet, he depicts a common experience of Indian life, showing the havoc caused by a river in flood. However, the context is broad enough to encompass the entire literary and cultural present and past of a people. On one level, there is a critique of both the old and the new. On the other hand, Tamil poets tend to romanticize floods, ignoring the suffering of the people. Ramanujan, by contrast, attempts to show how realistic poetry can be written on such topics. Additionally, the poet portrays the picture of his own ancestral home in his poem Small Scale Reflections on a Great House.

It is a memorable poem in which everything 'lost long ago' is revived in the speaker's memory. He gives The Great House a symbolic and cultural significance. The Great House stands for the undivided joint Hindu family, and the adjective 'Great' appears to be ironic, for there is nothing truly 'great' about it. It is here that identities are lost, swallowed up in the great mass of the family. According to Bruce King, the house is seen as the past, as memory, as tradition, as origin, offering different perspectives on it.

In fact, in many poems, Ramanujan demonstrates his modernity by placing the personal within a wider frame, such as the past and the present, to project an idea of continuity. To delineate experience in poetic terms, he prefers the imagistic and ironic mode. The imagistic mode helps the poet to convey in concrete terms what he thinks and feels; hence, his poetry is image-oriented. In poems like Breaded Fish, Love Poem for a Wife 1, Ecology, Routine Day Sonnet, Looking and Finding, Chicago Zen, History, Entry for a Catalogue of Fears, and A Poem on Particulars, we find him at his best in his use of images and symbols. Some poems, such as Self-Portrait, The Striders, and The Black Hen, follow the imagistic tradition.

To highlight A. K. Ramanujan's effective use of irony, Vilas Sarang rightly comments: "If one considers the ironic mode as the true modernist quality, then… Indian English poetry is modernist through and through" (Ed., 1980, Bombay: Disha Books).

To present a modern note of skepticism, Ramanujan cites many of his poems, such as *Obituary*, *History*, and *Snakes*. These poems reveal his skepticism towards the grandeur attached to tradition, death, history, ritual, and ceremonies. His perception of the superiority of body and soul in his old Hindu belief is discernible in the poem *A Hindu to His Body*, but he also shows his skeptical temperament in *Prayers to Lord Murugan*. His extremely scientific temperament is exemplified in his poem *Death and the Good Citizen*, while the seasons of the body, parallel to those in nature, are underlined in *In March*.

On the whole, as T. S. Eliot rightly affirms, no modern poet can dissociate himself from his past and tradition. In that sense, Ramanujan's modernity is profound and prolific, as it shows his acute awareness of tradition. Hence, he has a concrete base rooted in the personal or historical past, which enables him to present his modern sensibility, as seen in poems like *History*, *Obituary*, and *A River*.

To comment on A. K. Ramanujan's Indian-ness, Chidananda Das Gupta says that many writers like Ramanujan, although living abroad, carry with them an inner experience that they review, relive from time to time, and bring into contact with their present experiences, which nourishes their poetry. Thus, Ramanujan's poetry is permeated with Indian experience. Certainly, his poetry is an expression of Indian sensibility, sharpened and nourished by Western education and environment. Ramanujan himself writes (R. Parthasarathy, Ed., 1993, Oxford University Press, pp. 95, 96) in this connection:

> **"My first thirty years in India, My frequent visit and field trips My personal and professional Pre-occupation with Kannada, Tamil, the classics and folklore, give me my substance, My inner forms, images and symbols they are continuous with each other, And I can no longer tell what comes from where."**

Here, he observes complete artistic detachment and irony to portray the Indian scene from across the Atlantic. Certainly, Indian-ness has a universal appeal, which he portrays in his poetry. He feels at home in America, but his responses are entirely personal and differ from those of Americans. He explores India's common heritage of myth and tradition and is aware of the decadent social milieu of contemporary India.

He seeks his identity neither in America nor in the immediate present, but in the mythical and literary past. This means his success as a poet lies in the fusion of Indian sensibility with his American experiences. The East-West or the traditional-modern conflict provides the necessary tension in his poetry and raises it to the level of the best art. A. K. Ramanujan has abundantly drawn upon folklore to give him his 'inner form', 'images', and 'symbols'.

He explores India's common heritage of myth and tradition. The educated Indian faces a traumatic experience when he reviews India's tragic past against her equally tragic present. His predicament becomes truly tragic when he realizes that the perennial springs of tradition – myth, literature, and family – have become sterile. He is aware of the decadent social milieu of contemporary India.

There is much truth in the view that Ramanujan's poetry is dominated by five basic postulates, which we may call Indian-ness: i) Search for the self, ii) Family concerns, iii) Unified vision of life, iv) Myths and legends, and v) Peculiar Indian milieu.

His poetry is mainly dominated by his own self, reflecting his active concern with the dynamics of his sensibility – the precious stones, movements, and distinctions of his being as an individual and as an artist. In fact, this kind of concern with the self is found in all modern poetry.

In Ramanujan's case, poetry becomes inevitably a product of the interaction, interplay, and even the fusion of what he himself has called his inner and outer forms. These inner and outer forms are primarily responsible for his characteristic solipsism and his concern with the workings of his psyche. This is seen in his view of interpersonal relationships, nostalgia for the lost time of childhood, and the presence of parents, grandparents, and ancestral homes.

The self plays a significant role in Ramanujan's poetry. The poem *Self Portrait* not only illustrates a modern concern with the self but also the dramatic self, whose essential passivity allows it to resemble others over an intermediate stretch of time. This identification is important because it grants the self the freedom to share different identities and attitudes, each of them real in feeling and 'mysterious' in apprehension. In *Self Portrait*, the poet says: "I resemble everyone but myself." Here, the idea of the uniqueness of the individual soul is negated. The self is seen as linked with others, with everyone, and is influenced by the situation (the mirror in which it is viewed), shaped both by one's maker and by others. Hence, his *Elements of Composition* reinforces the idea that the individual self is meaningful only in relation to others – father, mother, uncle, sister, friends, and others.

Indian sensibility in Ramanujan finds its superb expression in poems dealing with familial relationships. Family and social concerns have always been at the center of Indian culture. They define and shape Indian-ness. According to R. Parthasarathy, family is one of the central metaphors with which Ramanujan thinks. Hence, in several of his poems, he explores both joint and nuclear families, as well as familial relationships, love, and marriage.

A different view of the self's attempt to seek fulfilment in family relationships can be found in his *Love Poem for a Wife, 1*. Here, the poet's nostalgia for the wife's 'unshared childhood' arises from his need to overcome the alienation that keeps them 'apart at the end of years.' The crisscross of memories and the enactment of the drama of the wife's past in the husband's consciousness only serve to emphasize the narrow limits within which the conjugal relationship appears to survive, with its explosive insecurities and tensions. The poem ends with the problematic uncertainty with which it began, implying that the husband's desire to start another life is bound to be frustrated.

Similarly, his poem *Small Scale Reflections on a Great House* is a memorable piece in which everything 'lost long ago' revives in the poet's memory, and he vividly describes the 'Great House,' closely related to his early life. The poet reflects on how a family attracts its different members. The entire description is nostalgic and has an Eliotian beginning: *"sometimes I think that nothing that ever comes into this house goes out."* The 'Great House' stands for the undivided joint Hindu family house, and the adjective *great* appears to be ironical, as there is nothing truly 'great' about it.

Because it is here that identities are lost, swallowed up in the great mass of family, the poet recollects familiar events and faces with which he was once very intimate. The comic and the pathetic, the humorous and the serious, are commingled.

Of Mothers, Among Other Things is another family poem by Ramanujan in which memory plays a vital part. Whether we call his family poems *"emotion recollected in tranquillity"* (Wordsworth's theory of poetry), or, as M. K. Naik puts it, his poetry originates from the past and is deeply rooted in his memory, the essence remains the same.

This poem tells the story of the poet's childhood recollections of his youthful mother at different stages of her life. The poet contrasts the youth of his mother with her old age. He is unable to convey the depth of his grief over her helplessness as she struggles to pick up a grain of rice from the floor with her crippled hand.

His next poem, *History*, exposes the greed within the family, describing how the daughter robs the great aunt. In contrast, *Love Poem for a Wife, I* depicts a psychic drama through the *'you'* and *'I'* conflict. It conveys the intensity of the poet's yearning for emotional fulfilment in familial relationships.

In *Still Another View of Grace*, he explores the conflict between East and West, past and present, tradition and modernity, using vivid, concrete images. He also evokes the figure of a seductive woman to whose passion he succumbs, despite his father's advice and the Brahmin tradition of his family. However, as a poet, he remembers his religious mother offering milk to cobras in *Snakes*.

His focus on his grandmother in poems like *Opposable Thumb* and *Lines to a Granny* establishes him as an excellent storyteller. We also encounter these qualities in *Obituary*, a poem about the poet's father, and *History*, a poem about several relatives.

Thus, it seems rather extraordinary that myth and history in Ramanujan's poetry are much discussed in literary circles. However, he lacks strength in both areas, and therefore, his metaphor of family never rises to a higher level of poetic significance. The clear and careful presentation of details in his poetry does not produce any extra dimension. In contrast, the same method in W. B. Yeats opens up a vast landscape and evokes a sense of discovery.

The Indian-ness of Ramanujan's poetry lies in his philosophical view of the oneness of life. One of his chief concerns is to perceive and establish a link between human beings and nature. As we know, Indians perceive a close affinity between human life and life in nature. For example, in "Looking for a Cousin on a Swing," the poem underlines the notion that the seeds of the present often lie in the past. It is a short poem that narrates a girl's memory of a particular childhood experience and the desire this memory arouses in her now, as she is growing up.

Here, the poet does not explicitly speak about the girl's sexual longing; rather, he suggests it. The male cousin is bound to experience a sexual desire, and that is what the girl actually wants, even though she does not articulate it. Thus, the poem sheds light on both child psychology and adult psychology.

"History" also shows that the present can shape the past, and that both are interlinked. This poem exposes the basic greed of all human beings. His poetry demonstrates how an Indian poet writing in English can draw strength from his roots. Thus, a 'single conversation' with his mother transforms him in the poem "History."

Hence, our view of history is subjective, whether familial or natural, and is constantly modified and altered through personal experience or study. The familial and natural experiences are essentially the same and subject to modification through the same process. In short, his vision of the past, present, and future is independent, yet projects the idea of continuity.

As a cosmopolitan poet, Rabindranath Tagore exemplifies how the Indian mind never hesitates to acknowledge its kinship with nature and its unbroken relationship with all. He observed a resemblance between the human body, the seasons, and the natural world, emphasizing their interconnectedness and simplicity. Similarly, Ramanujan's poem "Death and the Good Citizen" also explores the connection between the body and nature.

According to one critic, Ramanujan's poem *'A River'* about the Vaikai, which flows through Madurai, a city that has been the seat of

Tamil culture for nearly two thousand years, succeeds admirably in evoking the river. The critic adds that the river serves as a point of departure for ironically contrasting the relative attitudes of both old and new Tamil poets, who are exposed for their callousness to the suffering caused by the floods. Thus, the entire poem carries a distinctly Indian sensibility.

Another critic, M. Sivaramkrishnan, observes that for Ramanujan, history contemporizes itself largely through the intricate network of familial relations, with the figures of the father and mother dominating his interior landscape. While it is true that the range of subjects Ramanujan deals with in his poetry is somewhat limited, certain other qualities of his work compensate for this deficiency. His use of *myth and legend* plays a significant role in his poetic stance.

Indian sensibility is fundamentally mythic. Ramanujan's poetry is deeply rooted in Indian myths, legends, and rituals, though not in a celebratory tone or manner. An illustration of this can be found in his poem *'Snakes'*, which embodies the Hindu ritual of offering milk to snakes on *Nag Panchami Day*. In this ritual, the poet's mother belongs to that category of Hindu women who never kill a snake. On the contrary, they offer milk to snakes as part of a religious ceremony. This ritual reveals the large-heartedness and compassion of the Hindu mind.

In *'The Striders'*, we see Ramanujan's keen observational nature and his interest in the animal world. As in *'Snakes'*, the imagery in *'The Striders'* is also noteworthy. The diving of the water strider is suggestive of the diving of Vishnu's devotees into the depths of the water. Ramanujan uses the myth of Lord Vishnu and primeval water in the structure of the poem. The undertones of the myth illustrate the Indian idea that we all exist within the Lord, who is also within us.

Ramanujan also seeks the inner reality in a hesitant yet affirmative manner in his poem *'Prayers to Lord Murugan'*. Murugan is the name of the ancient Dravidian god of fertility, beauty, love, and war. His twelve eyes and six faces became for Ramanujan an ironic symbol of the comprehensiveness required to cope with the complex demands of reality. The concluding prayer in this poem, *'Lord of answers, cure us at once of prayers'*, releases the poet from the need for any further prayers, signaling a kind of spiritual resolution.

Thus, the poet employs the myth of Lord Murugan, a six-faced god with twelve hands. In this context, the lord is invoked for the death of old superstitions. Similarly, his poem *'Compensations'* contains an ironic reference to Lord Shiva and his *Tandava* dance. In this poem, the poet's ironic tone holds the lord responsible for all wars and other ills.

In Ramanujan's poetry, we find the typical Indian milieu effectively portrayed. It also reveals his essential Indian-ness more than anything else. His poem *'A River'* is an evocation of the river Vaikai, which flows through Madurai, a city that has long been the seat of Tamil culture. However, Ramanujan's sensibility remains deeply Indian. While his Western education and his time in the U. S. A. may have sharpened his sensibility, his connection to India and its culture remains profound. The poem also expresses his recollections of the past. Madurai is a city known for its temples and poets who have long celebrated it. The poet gives detailed descriptions of the wet and dry stones to portray the dry riverbed in summer. He contrasts this with the rising water levels and the way they carry off three village houses. The images of a 'pregnant woman,' loss of cattle, and the drowning of human lives are deeply significant.

It involves two generations: the present and the future. The image of 'identical twins' makes the loss more poignant. They are identical in their innocence, and the greatness of the poem lies in its traditional praise for the river as well as the poet's objective look at it. Thus, the language of the poem suits the theme well, and there is a definite touch of memorability about it.

Ramanujan wrote two poems, *'Love Poem for a Wife, 1'* and *'Love Poem for a Wife, 2'*, in which the poet harks back to his wife's unshared childhood. The first poem is rooted in the desire to overcome the alienation that keeps them "apart / at the end of years."

The poem is cleverly built on an ordinary, commonplace idea: that a man and a woman who get married to live together for the rest of their lives really don't know much about each other's pasts. They share each other's life after marriage, but what remains unshared forever is their childhood. Moreover, they don't know each other's parents well.

Thus, the poet tries to recall some of his wife's actions by recreating the past. This refers to the typical Indian betrothals that are arranged 'before birth' and marriages in *'Cradles'*. In *'Some Relations'*, he characterizes Indian thought in a way that only an Indian poet can. For instance, he says, "my daughter's unborn face floats to the surface."

Similar to this, Ramanujan's familial concern comes to the fore in his recollected memories of his father, mother, grandmother, and others, along with the various emotions that colour these family portraits. In *'Obituary'*, he tells us about the poet's father and hints at all that happens to a Hindu Brahmin family after the death of the patriarch. The poet's use of phrases like "debts and daughters," "bed-wetting grandson," and the list of things he has inherited – both assets and liabilities – calls attention to the historical and traditional aspects of Hindu culture.

Similarly, in *'Being the Burning Type'*, he performs all the religious rites as per Hindu ritual at the river, specifically the 'Sangam', where three rivers meet. This refers to the holy place of Allahabad, where the Ganges, the Yamuna, and the Saraswati meet, a site considered auspicious by Hindus. But at the end of the poem, the tone changes and takes on gravity when the poet mentions his mother in a melancholic mood, reflecting that he left them with a changed mother and more than one annual ritual.

Thus, Ramanujan presents a social picture through the *'Obituary'* of his father in an intimate manner. He follows the same trend of portraying the Indian milieu in his poems *'Small-Scale Reflections on a Great House'* and *'Of Mothers, Among Other Things'*. In *'The Great House'*, he presents the undivided joint Hindu family. In another poem, he recalls the childhood memories of his youthful mother and provides an 'objective correlative' of the emotion involved.

On the whole, to conclude on *Indian-ness*, one may affirm that Ramanujan's poems represent good Indian English poetry. In them, he portrays the joint Hindu family – a quintessentially Indian institution – that is now slowly disintegrating. He shows us how this system is fast breaking down, reflecting the decline of a once-strong tradition. These poems, then, not only depict our current social situation but also offer "hints and guesses" about the erosion of the familial and cultural structure.

Thus, his poetry offers insights into contemporary Indian life, inviting our participation in understanding the complexities of our identity. Ramanujan's greatness and his *Indian-ness* lie in his quest for self-identity, his focus on family, his unified vision of life, and his exploration of Indian myths, legends, and the peculiarities of Indian society.

For Ramanujan, alienation manifests in several ways. As a Brahmin, it is natural for him to feel alienated from an emerging secular, modern society. Additionally, as a Tamil-born poet living in a Kannada-speaking community, he experiences alienation in terms of cultural and linguistic identity. He also feels the tension between his early training in non-literary fields during the formative years of his education and his later immersion in the literary world.

Finally, he alienates himself through his decision to succeed in North America. This sense of alienation can be seen in his poems such as *Self Portrait*, *Conventions of Despair*, *Love Poem for a Wife, 1*, *Obituary*, *Zoo Gardens Revisited*, *Mythologies 1*, *Compensations*, *The Difference*, and *Small Scale Reflections on a Great House*.

According to Raghavendrarao, there are five types of alienation in the case of Ramanujan:

1. The alienation of the Brahmin Hindu orthodoxy family from modern society.
2. Linguistic isolation resulting from their adoption of English as the medium of their creative writing.
3. The alienation of a person trained in a non-literary realm.
4. Alienation arising from settling in America.
5. A universal alienation imposed by the Western dualistic worldview.

In addition, Raghavendrarao comments on Ramanujan's 'reverse romanticism', describing it as a poetic strategy that transforms the remote into the immediate. He also notes that Ramanujan relies on memory as a strategy to cope with his alienated condition. Indeed, alienation is a recurring theme in Ramanujan's poetry, and it becomes especially evident in poems such as *Self Portrait*, where he reflects on losing his identity and expresses his helplessness in this regard.

He ironically states that he resembles everyone except himself, appearing as a representative of the modern man who has lost his sense of anchorage. The loss of his roots is reflected in the distorted image of himself in the mirror. Instead of reflecting the poet's image, the mirror shows a portrait of a stranger, with the signature of the poet's father in the corner. The irony lies in the fact that the very preservation of his father's image in his memory makes the poet uneasy.

The loss of traditional values in the son is metaphorically represented by the distortion of his reflection in the mirror. The signature of his father serves as a reminder that traditional values cannot be easily or completely forsaken. Nissim Ezekiel's 'Self-Portrait' can perhaps be compared with 'Background, Casually' to reveal a similar sense of self.

Thus, the poet humorously refers to himself as "a poet-rascal-clown." His alienation is further explored in the poem 'Conventions of Despair', where the passive self, aware of its religious and cultural roots, completely rejects alienation and marginality. The poem explores the poet's struggle to reconcile his inner turmoil and his Hindu mind.

In other words, 'Conventions of Despair' witnesses a confrontation in the poet's mind between the modernity of American life and culture on one hand, and on the other, the orthodoxy of the Hindu faith, with its superstitious beliefs about the tortures sinners endure in hell.

To present *the presence of the past*, Ramanujan wrote his poem *Snake*. It is a poem in which the poet, most probably Ramanujan himself, recalls a childhood experience. This is a deeply personal and autobiographical poem, in which he describes how he eventually overcame his fear of snakes and could walk freely through the woods. Thus, it is clear that he transforms an ordinary past event – his mother offering milk to snakes – into something immediate and exotic.

However, one must also acknowledge that in many poems, such as *The Striders, Self Portrait*, and *No Man is an Island*, the poet does not resort to the strategy of reverse romanticism. Instead, he faces the immediate or the present as it is, and the experience is far from one of alienation. Similarly, his poem *Love Poem for a Wife, 1* reflects the self-attempt to seek fulfilment, but the alienation keeps the individuals apart.

To elaborate further, Ramanujan suggests that the only thing left for him is envy. In short, exile has certainly made a significant difference in him, and the alienation he suffers plays an important role in his poetic career. In Ramanujan's case, the experience of alienation is responsible for much of his detachment and objectivity.

To exemplify, alienation acquires a sort of desirability, and it also has a positive, creative side. Nissim Ezekiel, in his remarks on the alienation of Indo-English writers, suggests that alienation, while challenging, can be aesthetically productive and even desirable.

Ramanujan, too, has written three poems that highlight the self-deception of the Hindu. He clearly maintains a Hindu outlook, and perhaps his American experience led him to address this theme in several of his poems. For instance, in his work, he often adopts a detached attitude toward his cultural tradition from which he feels alienated.

These poems use irony to examine and critique this cultural tradition. They also mock the stereotypical image of the Hindu, who is portrayed as passive, calm, and detached, even in the face of the most severe provocation. This type of Hindu is so serene that he merely observes his wife enduring the worst of circumstances without taking action.

This type of Hindu is so calm that he merely watches his wife being raped by an enemy because he doesn't harm a fly or a spider. He reads his Gita, remains calm and detached, and treats the significant and the trivial equally. His three poems – The Hindu: He Doesn't Hurt a Fly or a Spider Either, The Hindoo: He Reads His Gita and Is Calm at All Events, and The Hindoo: The Only Risk – employ parallel frames. Essentially, all these poems highlight the fact that the self cannot fully reconcile with the inner life, which is known for its variety and depth.

However, his poem Conventions of Despair resolves with the poet's return to hell. In Chicago Zen, he appears to accept life's ordinariness and the karma of his nature. To express his deep-rooted Hindu outlook, he refers to a "monkey-temple" in an earlier poem.

His poems such as Obituary, Love Poem for a Wife, 1, Small-Scale Reflections on a Great House, History, Prayers to Lord Murugan, Snakes, and Mythologies 1, 2, 3 reflect ideas related to Hinduism. The detachment with which the poet offers his reflections on his great ancestral home is notable. While the poem Small-Scale Reflections on a Great House is suggestive of his tradition, past, and country, it also reveals the extent of his alienation.

As a poet, he vividly conjures up the image of the Great House connected to his early childhood through highly suggestive and evocative imagery, presenting the history of the ancient family and representing the concrete image of the Great House. Here, the house becomes a symbol of a vast joint family, where things that enter the house never leave. New things get completely absorbed into the older things, maintaining historic continuity. This means the past merges with the present. It is through this strategy that we uncover his essential alienation. However, in his poem *History*, we learn about the greed and callousness of his aunt's two daughters, which alters his perspective on the house. In *Obituary*, he speaks of "cremation," "ashes," and "priest" in the context of his father's death, while in *Small-Scale Reflections on a Great House*, he refers to Ganges water for the last rites of the dying.

Thus, the poet links the familial with the traditional and the historical by revealing his 'Hindu themes' as a part of his poetic philosophy. M. K. Naik (1981, *The Humanities Review*, Vol. 3, p. 15), a critic, concludes his note on alienation as: **"His poetry draws its sustenance. From the tension or the conflict in his mind between his intense Awareness**

of his Hindu heritage and the partly modernistic outlook which he has developed as a result of his prolonged contact with American culture." [7]

To sum up, he comments that his Hindu heritage does not lead to a blind acceptance of it on his part. He is equally aware of both the strengths and the deficiencies of his racial ethos. As we have seen, he admires in *Christmas*, and he recognizes the great absorbing power of Hinduism by describing a typical joint family in his poem *Small-Scale Reflections on a Great House*.

Thus, despite the obvious note of alienation, his poetry not only shows an intimate awareness of the Indian cultural and historical past but also reveals his alienation by questioning and undermining the Hindu religious tradition, values, and beliefs.

A. K. Ramanujan's poetry is largely autobiographical and reflective. His memories of his past, and especially of his relatives, figure prominently in his poems. He recalls his mother in the poem *Of Mothers, Among Other Things*, his father in *Obituary*, and his wife and several other relatives in *Love Poem for a Wife, 1*.

From this point of view, *Small-Scale Reflections on a Great House* is even more important because here he brings to life several of his relatives and sends one of them (a nephew) to his death. This poem is replete with his memories of the past, as the great house is his own ancestral home. The theme of 'family' is thus central to his poetry.

In the words of R. Parthasarathy, "family is one of the central metaphors with which Ramanujan thinks." This is self-evident from the titles of most of the poems included in *Relations*. According to S. Nagarajan, most of the poems in his second volume deal with his memories of his relations and the ambiguous freedom that life away from them confers. Additionally, critic M. K. Naik notes that Ramanujan's poetry is deeply rooted in family.

He constantly remembers with nostalgia the various members of his family, as well as the objects connected with his earlier life when he lived in India. In poem after poem, he returns to his childhood or boyhood experiences of life in southern India. These memories are recollected in the adult tranquillity of Chicago, with experiences imprinted on the mind of a sensitive, growing boy, pulsating back to life and entering his poems.

His self is the theatre in which incidents from the past are staged, and in which a number of people – such as his grandparents, mother, father, sister, and cousins – move and live again. Hence, one of the most important themes in his work is 'familial relations.' It is not a coincidence that even when he writes a poem unrelated to family relations, they still make their entry. Perhaps, for Ramanujan, as a poet, there is no self without familial relations, which becomes one of his central themes.

To explore his attempt to find fulfilment in family relationships, one may read his poem *Love Poem for a Wife, 1*. In it, we find different views of the self's attempt to seek fulfilment in familial connections.

Here, the poet's nostalgia for his wife's unshared childhood arises from his need to overcome the alienation that keeps them "apart at the end of years." However, the crisscross of memories, the enactment of the drama of the wife's past in the husband's consciousness, only serves to emphasize their narrow limits. Still, the conjugal relationship appears to survive its explosive insecurities and tensions. Hence, the poem ends with the same problematic uncertainty with which it began, implying that the husband's desire to start another life is bound to be frustrated.

As is well known, most of Ramanujan's poems originate from recollected personal emotions. They deal with the poet's memory of his relations and the freedom that life away from them confers. The sense of loss, as seen, is most powerfully connected with the mother, as shown in the poem *Of Mothers, Among Other Things*.

Though the family, for him, is one of the central metaphors with which he thinks, the intricacies of family relationships have been a major theme endlessly explored in Indian English poetry. As Daruwalla pointed out, "Perhaps, this has something to do with the strong family bond in India." (Cited in Dr. Satish Kumar/Tayal, Narain Series: Agra, p. 84)

Thus, in several of his poems, family and familial relations receive effective poetic treatment. Family becomes a springboard for him to project his varied viewpoints – philosophical and psychological – and to perceive continuity. He reacts differently to different aspects of domesticity or family through an ironic and imagistic mode of perception. The implicit irony in *Small-Scale Reflections on a Great House* undermines the greatness of the 'Great House' and the family, as seen in the image of "the girls hiding behind windows with holes in them." Here, the poet exposes the great house, which represents the undivided joint Hindu family, and the adjective 'great' appears to be ironic, for there is nothing truly 'great' about it. He also shows how a family attracts its different members. The poem has an Eliotian beginning. Thus, the poem dramatizes, in a mocking tone, the history of the great family house, which symbolically stands for India. In a way, the poet views the great house as the past, as tradition.

Parents figure prominently in several poems of Indo-Anglian poets. Mahapatra writes about his father and about himself as a father, while Gieve Patel has written beautiful poems about grandparents. However, it is probably A. K. Ramanujan who has explored these subjects more thoroughly and deeply than any other poet. His poetry is rich with references to his father, mother, grandmother, sister, wife, cousin, and others.

But all these impressions highlight family as the main concern of his poetry. *Obituary* is a poem in which the poet remembers his dead father and the legacy left for his son. The sad tone in the poem reminds one of *Forgive Me, Mother* by Eunice De Souza, who is also known for her poems on familial relations.

If the ironic mode is used to deflate the father's death in *Obituary*, the imagistic mode is used indirectly to evoke the poet's sense of grief for the helpless mother in *Of Mothers, Among Other Things*. The mother, thin and weak in old age, tries to pick up a grain of rice from the floor with her crippled hand.

Another example can be found in his poem *Looking for a Cousin on a Swing*. The poet searches for something vague and nostalgic. He remembers his childhood and that of his cousin, who was a playmate. They sat together on the swing, and every forward movement of the swing seemed to thrust their feelings into focus. The poet also draws a contrast between village life and town life and reflects on the prevailing tendency of people migrating to cities, abandoning all that is rustic.

In *History*, he takes up a past family event to show that history is composed of small events and is not constant. The present, with its new facts, reviews the past and reshapes it. This means the poet's view of history is completely altered when he learns that his aunt was one of the daughters who robbed her mother of her jewellery on her deathbed. Thus, he uses a family event not only to reveal the greed of some relatives but also to debunk the sentiments attached to the well-knit Hindu family in India.

However, in poems like *Love Poem for a Wife, 1*, he tries to understand the cause of disharmony in his marital relationship. His poems *Son to Father to Son* and *Drafts* most forcefully express his Indian view of parental relationships. In *In the Zoo*, he describes the scavenger bird. He also remembers his grandmother in poems like *Opposable Thumb* and *Lines to a Granny*. In *A Plant*, he suggests that nature can sometimes be cruel to the fauna on earth.

Finally, the same trend of writing to present the theme of family is evident in his other poems, such as *Looking and Finding*, *Chicago Zen*, *History*, *Relations*, *The Last of the Princesses*, *Snakes*, and others. He dwells on the theme of familial relations effectively. Thus, he establishes himself as a poet of familial relations and proves that family is a central metaphor in his poems.

As M. K. Naik rightly remarks, "Memory is not emotion recollected in tranquillity, but recollection emotionalized in un-tranquil moments, which appears to be the driving force behind much of Ramanujan's poetry" (1981, *The Humanities Review*, Vol. 3, p. 15).

He deals with memory as life seen through the eyes of a sensitive and observant boy growing up in a traditional middle-class Southern Hindu Brahmin family. His poetic self is always cautioned to maintain a distance from the memories, such that the subjective element of memory merges with the objective. His poetry is essentially the poetry of subjective experience, drawn from memories and impressions of a familial past.

His obsession with his past and his roots makes him rely heavily on memory, both as a theme and a poetic strategy. Memories of his mother, father, aunts, sisters, great-grandmother, grandfather, and a world of childhood and boyhood in a traditional South Indian Brahmin family are key characteristics of his poetry. According to him, creativity arises from sustained attention to one's own experience, one's own locality, and one's own landscape.

As many critics have pointed out, his inner world consists not merely of memories but also of fears and desires – such as the fear of snakes, sexual desire, the desire for unreflecting identity and harmony, and anxiety, which for him is a continuing process. For a complete understanding of his poetry, one must carefully study poems like *Small-Scale Reflections on a Great House*, *Some Indian Uses of History on a Rainy Day*, *Prayers to Lord Murugan*, *The Striders*, and *Love Poem for a Wife, 1*, among others.

It is significant that *Prayers to Lord Murugan* voices the poet's prayer to be delivered from both the weight of history and the abstractions of the modern world. Hence, the greatest strength of his poetry lies in its objectivity and poise, as well as the technical perfection that marks it throughout. His poetry is largely retrospective and reminiscent, with memory playing a significant role in shaping poetic experience.

Raghvendra Rao comes close to the truth when he says: "In Ramanujan, the problems of life and poetry are one and the same; it is the problem of uniting within a single poetic structure or life, memory as the past, memory as the present, and memory as the future" (M.K. Naik, 1982, *Madras: Macmillan*, p. 120, 125).

In other words, he continually looks back at his past life and writes poems about what stands out in his memory. Not all of his poems reflect nostalgic recollections of the past, as some of his experiences are unpleasant or depressing. In these poems, he relies solely on 'subjective memory,' while in others, he uses 'objective memory.' Only in a few poems does he succeed in fusing the two.

To justify this, M. K. Naik, a prominent critic, writes in his *History of Indian English Literature* that memory plays a vigorous, creative role in Ramanujan's poetry. This memory is fruitfully creative, attempting an almost total recall of sensuous childhood impressions – such as fear, sorrow, or death, as seen in *Snakes, Breaded Fish*, and *Opposable Thumb*. The role of memory is supremely narrated by him in poems like *History, Obituary, Looking for a Cousin on a Swing, Love Poem for a Wife, 1, Small-Scale Reflections on a Great House, Still Another View of Grace, A River*, and *Of Mothers, Among Other Things*, among others.

The poetic experience is largely determined by subjective or personal memory in poems like *History* and *Looking for a Cousin on a Swing* from the first volume, which reveal how childhood impressions, recalled years later, are understood from the vantage point of adult experience, yielding a surprising new perspective.

In this poem, the narrator is both an eyewitness and a reporter, recounting an incident that occurred on the day his great aunt died. The experience is transformed through time and exposure into an apparent pattern, which the narrator recalls years later, bringing to the poetic self the revelation that history, which usually changes slowly, can sometimes change in a single conversation. Thus, the memory is subjective, and an ordinary event is made to seem exotic. However, on the whole, the experience fails to appeal to us in any subtle or profound way.

In *Obituary*, the poet deals with another personal memory, focusing on the death of his father. Here, we are told that the father, as a common man, left nothing for the family except "debts and daughters," "a changed mother," a bed-wetting grandson, and a lean house. The two-line obituary in a Madras newspaper attempts to capture the poet's strategy of making the extraordinary seem like the ordinary. The tone of the poem is comic, ironic, and non-romantic, offering a poignant hint at the essential absurdity of life and its memory.

His next poem, *Of Mothers, Among Other Things*, offers a series of images of carefully preserved memories. He recalls the pleasant sight of his mother with her earrings, each with "three diamonds splashing a handful of needles," and later, when she was weak and thin. One of her hands was crippled, making it difficult for her to pick up even a grain of rice from the floor with her "four still-sensible fingers." Here, the memory remains confined to the subjective self.

Looking for a Cousin on a Swing seems to be a more impersonal poem. A third person describes the experiences contained in this poem. Certainly, it is a backward-looking piece written in a nostalgic mood. The poet is in a reminiscent state, cherishing the memory of a cousin who was once his playmate when they were children. She was four or five years old, and he was about two years older than her. He remembers how, with age, their bodies became flabby.

In addition to this, he has written *A River* and *Of Mothers, Among Other Things* in an impersonal or objective manner, where memory is used to fuse the present and the past. It is no longer a loss in time. *A River* is a poem about the Vaikai River, which flows through Madurai, a city long known as the seat of Tamil culture. The poem is an evocation of the river.

The poet clearly reveals the attitudes of both old and new Tamil poets, who have shown utter indifference and callousness to human suffering during the time of a devastating flood. Here, the poet uses his past memory of his visit to Madurai, the city of temples and poets, through which the Vaikai River flows, to connect the present with the cultural-historical past.

When he was in Madurai for a day, the river was in flood, and he learned about the havoc it caused everywhere. He went down memory lane and placed himself in the Tamil cultural past, when poets sang only of the floods, ignoring the hardships faced by the common people. Memory in this poem, thus, serves as a poetic strategy to link the past with the present and project the idea of continuity.

In *The Last of the Princesses*, Ramanujan relies on what we call "objective memory." Through some well-etched images, he shows the decline and fall of the great Mughal dynasty. Throughout the poem, as a poet, he uses memory in a cultural-historical context. The 'rickshaw-wallah' maintains an objective attitude and an objective manner, reflecting the detachment in the narrative.

His ironic tone highlights the plight of the poor rickshaw-wallah. In contrast, in his poem *A Hindu to His Body*, he uses memory in an objective manner within a wider framework of time. The body is left behind by the soul upon death.

According to common Hindu belief, in this poem, a Hindu asks his body not to abandon him, that is, not to leave his soul behind. It was the body that brought him into the world, endowed him with different feelings, and made him perform acts of love and hatred. In this poem, the poet seems to succeed in resolving the conflict between the past and the present by linking them together through memory.

Similarly, his poem *Still Another View of Grace* describes a past experience that is nostalgic. Even though the poet feels morally guilty about deviating from the path of virtue, having yielded to the temptation of sex with a streetwalker, the poem reflects this inner conflict. Poems like *Snakes* and *Breaded Fish* are also retrospective, personal, and autobiographical.

There is nothing wistful about that experience, though there may be a touch of wastefulness in the relief the poet feels after getting rid of his fear of snakes. In Still Life, however, he certainly expresses a desire to meet once again the woman who has just left, leaving behind only the shape of her bite on the half-eaten sandwich and the salami.

Thus, memory plays an extremely important role as a poetic strategy in Ramanujan's poetry. However, it would be wrong to say that he completely ignores the immediate and the present. In his first volume, memory often highlights the little ironies of life, while in his second volume, through memory, he portrays great moments of anguish and loss.

CHAPTER-4

A.K. Ramanujan's Thematic Concern

A noted critic Vilas Sarang has rightly quoted about Ramanujan's use of Irony in his poem as: **"If one considers the ironic mode, as the true modernist quality then Indian English poetry is modernist through and through,"**[1] (Ed.,1990,Disha Book: Bombay)

Irony is perhaps the most prominent quality of his poetry. In this regard, we might even place him above Nissim Ezekiel. The modern Indian English poet, it seems, heavily relies on irony. Kolhatkar, Daruwalla, Patel, and Sharat Chandra all write poetry saturated with irony. While the ironic mode is considered the supreme poetic path, as Sarang puts it, poets also use irony for comic effects. However, Ramanujan uses it to emphasize the melancholy, gloom, and pessimism of his poems. Almost every poem of his is characterized by irony to some degree.

Perhaps the first poem, "Looking for a Cousin on a Swing," contains a touch of irony when the poet describes the little girl recalling her experience on the swing with her cousin. The irony deepens when the poet says that she looks for the swing in cities and tries to remain innocent about it. What the poet wishes to convey is that there is something exotic about it. In "A River," the poem begins with a realistic description of the Vaikai River in Madurai, a seat of Tamil culture and a centre of great learning. However, the poem ironically exposes the callousness of both old and new poets who are blind to the havoc caused by the floods. Here, the poet aims to convey the idea that poets write about the damage and flooding of the river. It is ironic that the river fills with water only once a year.

Ramanujan's "*Love Poem for a Wife, I*" is notable for the ironic twist at the end. Irony pervades the poem throughout. There is irony in the poet's reference to his wife's seven crazy aunts, particularly in his use of the word "Mythology," as they were merely an invention of his wife. Another ironic element arises when he refers to his wife's father, her brother James, and her, as they are the targets of his ironic attacks. As seen in the earlier poem, irony also permeates *Small Scale Reflections on a Great House*. The poem has an Eliotian beginning, meaning the poet, Ramanujan himself, ironically states that things come every day. Yet, it is even more ironic that lame, wandering cows, coming to this house from nowhere, have been known to be tethered, while the girls hide behind windows with holes in them. Furthermore, the example of the beggar, "a prostitute song," adds another layer of irony. When the poet says that the daughters of this family marry short-lived idiots, and that the sons run away from home only to return with grandchildren, reciting Sanskrit to approving old men, it is filled with irony. This poem is, indeed, steeped in irony.

Another notable example of an entirely ironic poem is *Obituary*. It is quite ridiculous when the poet, Ramanujan himself, laughs at his own father, who, at his death, left behind "debts and a daughter" and also "a bed-wetting grandson," named after him by the toss of a coin. The poet describes his father as being of the 'burning type' and states that he "burned properly at the cremation." The irony deepens when the poet reflects on his father's birth, which occurred through a Caesarean operation in a Brahmin ghetto, and his death by heart failure in a fruit market. However, the most significant irony is when the poet says that his father left behind "a changed mother" with "more than one annual ritual."

In a similar vein, Ramanujan's use of irony can be observed in poems such as *Still Another View of Life* and *Conventions of Despair*. In the first poem, he ironically critiques the conventional code of morality, which ignores the realities of human nature. Yet, in reality, he is well aware of what modernity entails and why he cannot completely discard his orthodox Hinduism. Modernity, according to the poem, requires things like remarrying, going to the movies, and visiting a psychoanalyst. The closing line of this poem also underscores the use of irony.

In short, irony has been a powerful device in the hands of Ramanujan, and it is almost all-pervasive, especially in his poems about familial relations. He exemplifies this in works such as *Still Life*, *Self-Portrait*, *Image for Politics*, *Relations*, and *Conventions of Despair*, where irony becomes a defining feature.

Ramanujan's poetry is image-oriented, as Satyanarain Singh notes, and he is correct. His genius seeks the particular, the precise, and the concrete, as opposed to the general, the vague, and the abstract. This focus on specificity is evident even in the titles of his poems, such as *The Striders*, *Snakes*, *Breaded Fish*, *Ecology*, *Routine Day Sonnet*, *Looking and Finding*, *Chicago Zen*, *History*, and *Of Mothers, Among Other Things*. Ramanujan has a keen eye for the unique physiognomy of objects and an insightful understanding of their characteristic qualities.

His imagery carries within it the precise form of objects, along with a vivid sense of their distinctive qualities. For instance, in *The Striders*. According to the same critic, Ezekiel's poetry is more thought-oriented and rarely strong in imagery, whereas, in the case of these two poets, the image surpasses the idea in Ramanujan's poetry, while in Ezekiel's, the idea eludes the image. This contrast is evident in his poem *Poet, Lover, and Bird Watcher*.

Ramanujan's poems are well known for their unforgettable images, innovations in language, depictions of familial relations, ironic descriptions, Hindu themes, Indian-ness, nostalgia, fear, anxiety, and many other themes. This article focuses on a selection of his poems, as only a few are considered here.

An analysis of these poems reveals that his genius primarily seeks the particular, as opposed to the general. His craftsmanship with language and imagery is undeniable. The images in his poetry are unique in that they carry the precise forms of objects with a vivid sense of their distinctive qualities. In this respect, he is closer to Keats than to Shelley.

It has been observed that in Ramanujan's poetry, the image surpasses the idea. In this regard, he has sometimes been contrasted with Nissim Ezekiel, in whose poetry the idea often eludes the image. This concreteness and precision are achieved through the use of vivid, visual, and telling images. His poetry is "image-oriented," where the image serves not only as the springboard for poetic composition but also as the very core of the poem.

According to Parthasarthy: **"The images are primarily visual words tend to collocate together into an image which they trigger off the Poem, the entire poem is, in fact, one image or a complex of more than one image, it is in this context that the use of the image is seminal."**[2] (1993, O.U.P.:N.D., Cit. Opt)

A. K. Ramanujan has also employed various categories of images, giving his poetry the power to evoke the multi-dimensional experience of life. Often, the images are complex, capable of arousing both visual and auditory sensations simultaneously. For instance, in *Snakes*, he writes: "The twirls of their hisses / rise like tiny dust cones on slow-noon roads winding through the farmers' feet." (A. K. Ramanujan, 1966, Vol. I)

Here, the images of the slow-noon roads and the farmers walking along those roads are both vivid and realistic. Along with this visual image, we also have the auditory image of the hissing of snakes. This blending of visual and auditory imagery is a frequent feature of Ramanujan's poetry. Sometimes, he creates tableau-like effects, as seen in poems such as *Still Life* and *A River*. These poems highlight not only his eye for detail but also his ability to depict scenes with photographic fidelity. We find examples of such cameo-like images in poems like *Poona Train Window* and *Some Indian Uses of History on a Rainy Day*.

Another distinctive feature of his imagery is its structural quality. The organization of a poem by Ramanujan can often be studied in terms of the pattern of images. This is especially noticeable in poems such as *The Striders* and *Still Life*.

A. K. Ramanujan's realistic and vivid imagery is one of the foremost merits of his poetry. Undoubtedly, it is his strength, although his imagery does have its weak points. One of the best examples of this is his poem *Of Mothers, Among Other Things*. In this poem, he depicts, through graphic imagery, the youthfulness of a woman, her maturation into motherhood, and her subsequent flabbiness and loose flesh.

Thus, we see the mother in our imagination almost exactly as Ramanujan has depicted her. However, it must be pointed out that some of his imagery, particularly in this poem, is vague, incoherent, and even confusing. For instance, we can clearly visualize the silk and white petal of the mother's youth, with her three diamonds sparkling and radiating light. We can also visualize a wet eagle's twisted claws; however, it is unclear whether the crippled talon belonged to the eagle, caught in a garden trap, or if it was one of the mother's fingers, which was hurt and rendered ineffective after being trapped in the garden.

In the closing three lines, it becomes clear that it was the mother's finger that was rendered ineffective and un-operational. The poet recalls seeing her four still-sensible fingers picking up a grain of rice from the kitchen floor. This final image has the merit of being both realistic and vivid. It also includes the image of the mother's sari, no longer clinging to her body but hanging loose, reflecting her old age and the loss of firm flesh.

To further highlight Ramanujan's extensive use of images, one may consider the following poems. In his much-discussed poem *The Striders*, the insect – a type of water bug – is vividly brought to life. The picture of the bubble-eyed water bugs, "Perching weightless on the ripple skin of a stream," is realistically portrayed, and the image evokes a spiritual dimension. To commemorate it, Ramanujan writes, "No, not only prophets walk on water, this bug sits in a landslide of lights and drowns eye-deep into its tiny strip of sky." (A. K. Ramanujan, Vol. I, 1966)

This description brings to mind Arun Kolhatkar's poem *The Butterfly*, where the poet suggests that the butterfly has no future. *A River* is another poem that draws attention for its meticulous use of imagery. The images of "women's hair clogging the watergates," "wet stones glistening like sleepy crocodiles," and "shaven water buffalo and pregnant woman" are just a few of the vivid images that keep the poem lively and true to life.

One can observe a similar effect in Daruwalla's *River-Silt* and note Keats's influence in Ramanujan's *Obituary*. The latter poem also abounds in visual imagery, such as "the house that leaned" and "the bent coconut tree," which evoke realistic pictures in the reader's mind. Additionally, he mentions "the dust on a table full of papers" and the "bed-wetting grandson," further enhancing the vividness of his depiction.

Similar to this, one may be reminded of D. H. Lawrence's *Snakes*, which is notable for its lifelike imagery. Both poems are rich in visual images. In fact, the earth-brown, earth-golden snake in Lawrence's poem symbolizes the mysterious forces of nature unknown to man. In *Looking for a Cousin on a Swing*, Ramanujan uses visual symbols like 'fig tree,' 'climbing,' and 'swinging' as symbols of the Garden of Eden. The little girl was four or five, and her cousin was six or seven, much like the figures in the fig tree. This recalls the innocence and joy that Adam and Eve enjoyed in paradise. The fig tree of their childhood later becomes a symbol of experience.

In short, the images of the past represent innocence, while those of experience reflect their village and metropolitan lives. His fondness for visual and other types of images is revealed in many of his other poems as well. For example, *Hindu to His Body* visualizes the body as the image of the soul, and *A Plant* is filled with visual imagery.

To sum up, Ramanujan deserves high praise for his mastery of the English language and image-oriented poetry. While it is rare to find a poet whose work does not contain imagery, and often in abundance, Ramanujan's imagery possesses certain qualities that distinguish it from that of other poets.

According to the eminent critic M. K. Naik, Ramanujan fully exploited the opportunities presented by his Hindu heritage and the memories of his early life. Through this, he was able to articulate the Hindu ethos in his poetry. His work is not merely peripheral to the core of the Hindu experience; however, he was certainly influenced by Western life and culture as well as the traditions of Hinduism, the religion to which he belonged.

The cultural values of Hinduism always remained with him, leading to a kind of uneasy tension between the modernity of Western culture and the orthodoxy of ancient Hindu traditions. This tension, in turn, found expression in his poetry. Perhaps, Ramanujan had yet to fully reconcile this duality within himself. Nevertheless, he was able to demonstrate to his contemporaries the supreme importance of having roots and also provided glimpses of the vitality that a poet's work acquires from such a connection.

Ramanujan's Hindu heritage greatly influenced his poetry, and it is a theme that occupies a central place in his work. As R. Parthasarthy remarks, "His poetry draws its sustenance from his intense awareness of his racial burden – his Hindu heritage" (O.P. Bhatnagar, Jaipur: Rachana Prakashan, pp. 107).

In his poem *Conventions of Despair*, Ramanujan states that he finds his hell in his Hindu mind, a statement that he regards as a central motto in his poetry. However, he does not accept his Hindu heritage blindly. He is keenly aware of both the strengths and the deficiencies of his racial ethos. For instance, in his poem *Small Scale Reflections on a Great House*, he portrays a typical Hindu family, acknowledging the great absorbing power of his Hindu faith.

At the same time, Ramanujan does not overlook the limitations of Hinduism in fully satisfying the modern mind, which often perceives the presence of primitive or elemental evil in human life. In contrast, his poem *Hindu Reading His Gita* illustrates a sense of calmness that ultimately breaks down in times of crisis.

This juxtaposition of the ancient Hindu ethos with the modern Hindu experience is further explored in his poem *Some Indian Uses of History on a Rainy Day*. Additionally, in *Christmas*, he contrasts the Hindu worldview with that of the Western perspective. By blending themes of family and Hindu heritage, Ramanujan creates an interesting and complex mix in many of his poems. In *Self-Portrait*, he reflects on his image in the mirror as that of a stranger, and in *Relations*, he evokes ancestral crocodiles and tortoises, adding layers to his exploration of identity and heritage.

To conclude, it can be affirmed that poems like *Still Another View of Grace*, *Christmas*, and *Some Indian Uses of History on a Rainy Day* explore the tension between Ramanujan's strong sense of Hindu heritage and the intrusion of modern values into his sensibility, which constitutes a central theme of his work.

Both A. K. Ramanujan and Nissim Ezekiel have written love poems, but Ramanujan's love poetry is much less satisfactory than Ezekiel's. His love poems are not the kind that one can easily admire. A critical study of his entire body of work does not categorize Ramanujan as a poet of love for several reasons. First, he has written very few poems specifically about love, and these are often not conventional love poems. While his treatment of love is, on the whole, cerebral like that of other poets, Ramanujan does not start with a genuine personal experience. Though his love poetry holds its own validity, it remains somewhat limited in scope.

To exemplify this, A. K. Ramanujan expresses the view that an unshared childhood separates a husband and wife, and that had they shared a similar childhood, they might have led a happier conjugal life. While this may not be a very convincing explanation of the problem, in his poem *Two Styles in Love*, he presents two imaginary lovers responding to each other's manners of love. In his last anthology, Ramanujan wrote six poems entitled *Love Poem 1 to 6*, portraying different viewpoints and situations in love quite realistically. However, in all these poems, the mock-ironic tone often undercuts the intensity of the burning passion of love. For instance, a short poem titled *Still Life* seems to celebrate love as an abiding experience, although the idea is expressed rather vaguely.

According to a critic, both these poems are notable for their quiet yet deep emotion, their fine perception, and their treatment of love, which is one of the most basic human experiences. In this regard, the critic may be right. *Looking for a Cousin on a Swing* is also regarded as a love poem by some. However, Ezekiel's love poems fail to elicit a strong enough emotional response from the reader, and they cannot be considered truly memorable love poems. Therefore, neither Ramanujan nor Ezekiel has written a love poem that can be described as truly lyrical in inspiration and in its treatment of the passion of love.

To illustrate his portrayal of marital love, A. K. Ramanujan has analyzed poems such as *Love Poem for a Wife, 1 & 2* and *Love Poem for a Wife and Her Trees*. In the first poem, he stages a powerful psychic drama through the voices of 'you' and 'I'. There is a crisscross of memories, which effectively conveys the intensity of the poet's yearning for emotional fulfilment in family relationships. The family figures and relationships become symbols for the expression of the poet's emotions.

At the end of the poem, the poet suggests that sharing childhood experiences is essential for emotional fulfilment in marital life. To make this possible, he ironically proposes two alternatives. First, people may follow the example of Queen Cleopatra of Egypt, who married her own brother and shared each other's childhood experiences, a common social practice in ancient Egypt. Alternatively, they could follow the custom of child marriage.

In *Love Poem for a Wife, 2*, however, the sense of estrangement disappears, and the tone becomes softer, as in *Still Another View of Grace*. The intellect, or logic, aids the poetic self in bridging the emotional gap, to such an extent that the poet-husband even gains a glimpse into his wife's childhood. Additionally, it can be said that here, the poet identifies the cause of the disharmony as the difference in their cultural backgrounds. This cultural gap, along with the bitter nature of the wife, keeps the husband tense and haunted by strange dreams. In one of his dreams, he identifies his face with his wife's, which makes him realize the need for harmony and integration.

Ramanujan follows the same trend in *Love Poem for a Wife and Her Trees*. It represents an awareness of accepting the situation as it is and explores the theme of alienation within a marital relationship. Thus, in all the poems addressed to his wife, the tone ultimately ends on a note of compromise, much like love poems in the tradition of Eliot's *The Love Song of J. Alfred Prufrock*.

A. K. Ramanujan also strikes a metaphysical note of realism in his love poetry. Though *Obituary* is written in a mock-ironic tone, and his use of irony is very subtle, the poem exposes the futility of social customs, which are often very expensive. However, it is only the loving son, like Ramanujan, who remembers even the insignificant events of his father's life due to deep love and reverence.

Thus, Ramanujan achieves universality in his love poetry by inventing situations, adorning his expressions with masks, and avoiding a flat tone. His strategy of maintaining control over his emotions through irony deprives his love poetry of intensity and, in some cases, even authenticity. Consequently, his love for his deceased father remains concealed in a mock-ironic narrative. In poems like *Of Mothers, Among Other Things*, he communicates his impressions of his mother at various stages of her life through evocative imagery. The language of this lyric is precise and clear, with apt diction and vivid visual images that set it apart as a charming piece.

No doubt, Ramanujan is a love poet when considering his morphogenetic inheritance, which includes Tamil and its great traditions of love poetry. His translations such as *Speaking of Siva, The Interior*

Landscape, *Poems of Love and War*, and *The Hymns for the Drowning* draw heavily on this tradition of spiritual love.

By any standard, Ramanujan has crafted classic love poems with metaphysical dimensions, where relationships are portrayed through the metaphors of trees, stems, branches, and twigs. His love poetry, thus, carries a certain terrible beauty and passion. The fusion of English, with its outer forms, and his native Tamil, with its inner forms, infuses his poetry with a unique beauty. However, the absence of genuine personal feeling and his avoidance of direct emotional expression leave his love poetry somewhat sterile.

There is considerable truth in the view that A. K. Ramanujan's poetry is dominated by his self. His work is largely retrospective and reflective, focusing on his personal experiences, memories, and inner world. The essence of his poetry lies in his exploration of his own sensibility – capturing the subtleties, movements, and unique aspects of his being both as an individual and as an artist. This emphasis on self is a common characteristic of much modern poetry, where poets often turn inward to examine their thoughts, emotions, and perceptions.

The poetic quality of Ramanujan's work is evident in his choice of subject matter and his remarkable ability to condense complex ideas through precise language. His skillful use of words, combined into evocative phrases, clauses, and sentences, adds depth to his poems. The incidental details he weaves into his poetry further enhance its richness, drawing readers into the nuanced world he presents. These details not only add interest but also contribute to the poem's overall artistic quality.

This attention to detail and depth is also present in his prose. Though his prose is straightforward, it is packed with suggestions and layers of meaning, often pushing the boundaries of its own form.

Ramanujan has always been recognized as a keen observer of the world around him, capturing the ordinary and transforming it into something profound.

In several of his poems, Ramanujan shines as a societal critic. He doesn't shy away from critiquing not just society at large but also his own community, including fellow poets. His poetry often touches on familial relationships, with recurring references to his father, mother, grandmother, sister, wife, and cousin. The concept of 'family' is central to much of his work, reflecting his deep concern with personal connections and the complexities of familial bonds.

Finally, Ramanujan deserves recognition for his mastery of the English language. Though a native of India, he brought a unique blend of cultural richness and linguistic dexterity to his poetry. His ability to craft vivid imagery, nuanced emotions, and incisive observations in English allows him to reach a wide audience, earning him a place among the most distinguished poets of his generation.

A. K. Ramanujan's poetry is rich with felicities of words and phrases, demonstrating his exceptional command of language. He is known for writing primarily in free verse, often eschewing punctuation, which gives his poetry a flowing, organic quality. Despite this freeform style, he skilfully incorporates rhyme and assonance, adding musicality and rhythm to his work. Critics often commend Ramanujan for his craftsmanship, appreciating the way he balances the structure of language with the emotional depth he conveys.

In his poem *'A River'*, Ramanujan offers a poignant commentary on humanity and human suffering. He subtly critiques poets – both ancient and contemporary – for their focus on idealized themes such as cities and temples, often neglecting the lives of ordinary people. Through this irony, he emphasizes upon the disconnect between poetic tradition and the real, often painful experiences of everyday life. Rather than offering a traditional song of praise for the river, Ramanujan focuses on the villagers' actual experiences, portraying a more authentic and human-cantered view of life. The poem is narrated from the perspective of an outsider or visitor, using the language and perspective of a common villager to present an objective, grounded account.

In *'Of Mothers, Among Other Things'*, memory once again plays a central role. This family poem reflects Ramanujan's deep engagement with personal and familial histories, where memory shapes the way the past is understood and presented. The poem delves into the stages of a mother's life, using vivid imagery and emotional resonance to convey the passage of time and the transformations that accompany it. Through his exploration of memory, Ramanujan captures both the universal and personal aspects of human existence, connecting readers to shared experiences of love, loss, and family.

In A. K. Ramanujan's poetry, particularly in the poem *'Love Poem for a Wife, 1'*, the metaphor used in the first two lines captures the difficulty and futility of trying to articulate the rough, bitter taste of past memories. This metaphor suggests the limitations of language in fully conveying emotional depth, particularly when it comes to personal experiences like love or regret. The poet uses the concept of 'objective-correlative' – a literary technique coined by T.S. Eliot – where external objects or events serve to evoke specific emotions in the reader. In this poem, the past actions of the wife are recalled and recreated, yet there is an implicit sense of disconnection between the speaker and his wife, reflecting the broader theme that it is nearly impossible to truly enter into someone else's life or understand their experiences fully.

The poem can be seen as a satire on the act of choosing a life partner and the subsequent realization that one cannot share each other's past experiences. It highlights the emotional distance that remains even in close relationships, despite efforts to reconnect with the past.

In contrast, Ramanujan's *'Small Scale Reflections on a Great House'* offers a critical commentary on the traditional joint Hindu family system. The poem discusses the "Great House," which, while seemingly grand, is ironically depicted as anything but great. The large, undivided family structure, where individual identities are often swallowed up in the mass of familial obligations, is exposed as a site of stagnation and loss. The 'Great' in the title serves as an ironic commentary on the fading significance of the traditional family system. Ramanujan subtly critiques the joint family structure, presenting it as a space where individual lives and desires are often subsumed by collective expectations and obligations.

This poem is a poignant reflection on the contemporary decline of the joint Hindu family system, an institution that once provided stability and structure but is now undergoing fragmentation. The poem invites readers to reflect on their own experiences with family dynamics and consider the shifting social fabric of modern India. Ramanujan's ability to address such personal yet universal themes makes this a significant contribution to Indian English poetry, encapsulating the cultural and social changes of the time.

A. K. Ramanujan's poem *'Obituary'* explores the aftermath of a patriarch's death, portraying both the personal and societal rituals that follow. The poem touches on a significant Hindu tradition of immersing the ashes of the deceased in a river, particularly referencing the sacred *Sangam* where rivers meet. Through the use of references to everyday objects like 'stones,' the 'grocery shop,' 'street hawker,' and an 'annual ritual with changed mother,' Ramanujan gives us a glimpse of the mundane yet profound transformations that occur in a family after a death. His depiction of these rituals is both poignant and social, intertwining personal loss with the cultural practices that shape the community.

The *'Obituary'* also exemplifies Ramanujan's skill in blending levity with seriousness. The poem shifts in tone from reflective and solemn to more conversational and casual. This modulation of tone serves to create a layered narrative that speaks to both the emotional gravity of death and the practical realities of daily life. By invoking a conversational rhythm, the poem takes on an intimate quality, making the reader feel as if they are engaged in a direct dialogue with the poet. This creates a sense of familiarity, allowing readers to connect with the emotions and rituals described, ultimately making the poem a deeply evocative reflection on loss, memory, and cultural practice.

In *'The Last of the Princess'*, Ramanujan examines the tragic decline of the Mughal Empire through the lens of its last princess, portraying her suffering and poverty. This poem reflects on the impermanence of power and wealth, emphasizing the slow disintegration of the empire and its once-glorious past. The poet uses the figure of the princess as a symbol of the empire's fall, focusing on the loss of dignity and the stark reality of poverty that follows.

The poem *'Conventions of Despair'* further highlights Ramanujan's complex relationship with both Indian and Western traditions. Influenced by Western education, Ramanujan's speaker finds himself caught between rejecting both the modern and traditional Hindu conventions of despair. The poem reflects the existential tension of modern Indian sensibility – caught between a Westernized understanding of the world and an enduring attachment to ancient, archaic forms of despair. The poet grapples with this duality, ultimately presenting an emotional and intellectual response to the dilemmas posed by modernity and tradition.

Through these poems, Ramanujan delves into personal and societal themes with depth and sensitivity. His exploration of cultural rituals, personal loss, and the complexities of modern identity offers readers a rich tapestry of thought, emotion, and critique. His works often blur the lines between the personal and the universal, highlighting the intricate ways in which individual lives are intertwined with broader cultural and historical forces.

In conclusion, A. K. Ramanujan's poetry moves from personal experience to a broader, collective experience, seeking comfort and solace in the rich heritage of his community's past. By delving into India's mythological and traditional roots, he connects his personal identity to the larger cultural fabric of his heritage. However, despite his connection to tradition, Ramanujan also reflects on the challenges of modernity. He critiques the alienating aspects of modern life, which, in his view, can render individuals like himself as 'Marginal Men,' caught between the pull of the past and the demands of the present. Thus, while the poet recognizes the necessity of embracing modernity, he ultimately condemns it, seeing it as a realm where he, and others like him, are pushed to the margins of society.

CHAPTER-5

A.K. Ramanujan's Poetic Craftsmanship

Chicaned Das rightly acclaims, "It is not obvious the poet in Ramanujan but it has discovered gradually." (Satish Kumar/Anupam Tayal, Narain Series: Agra, p. 78, Opt., and cited) Attippat Krishna Swami Ramanujan, a Tamil Brahmin Hindu, rejected Hindu orthodoxy and its decadent values and beliefs. As a cosmopolitan, he read the poetry of T.S. Eliot, Dylan Thomas, and the famous Kannada poet, Adiga. A major turning point in his career came when he earned a graduate diploma in linguistics. His Fulbright fellowship enabled him to go to the United States, where he became a full-fledged professor before his sudden death in 1993. Ramanujan's first marriage, to a Syrian Christian woman, Molly Daniel, ended in divorce. Thus, throughout his life, he remained influenced by Buddhism.

A. K. Ramanujan, one of the big three of Indo-English poets, is often mentioned alongside Nissim Ezekiel and Kamla Das. Although his poetic output consists of only a few slender volumes, he was a subtle and genuine poet. His poetry is celebrated for its striking modernity and realism. There is no doubt that some of his poems follow the best traditions of modern Western poetry. However, his voluntary settlement in the United States bound him to North America, where he made a significant mark.

To express his sense of alienation, at least in some of his poems, R. Parthasarathy cites a quote from Kulshrestha: "He was alone among his peers in cultivating a uniquely personal idiom, which reflected his involvement with the problem of self-definition, perhaps more artistically viable than that of others" (1980, opt., cit., Arnold Heinemann: N.D.). His alienation manifested in multiple ways. Initially, his alienation as a Brahmin and from his country caused him distress, but it later propelled him into the literary world. The best example of this is his poem *Self Portrait*, which resembles Nissim Ezekiel's *Background, Casually*; both reveal a self-alienated from its own observer.

According to A. K. Ramanujan, his knowledge of English, linguistics, and anthropology provided him with 'outer' forms – linguistic, metrical, logical, and others. These forms shaped his experiences, and his first thirty years in India, his frequent visits and field trips, and his personal and professional involvement with Kannada, Tamil, and the classics and folklore provided him with the 'inner' forms – images and symbols. Thus, English and Tamil were complementary to each other, and his oldest concerns were the form of his poetry. The content did not exist independently; the meaning changed with the form. The most profound thoughts, according to him, emerged in a particular form that embodied them. Therefore, critics have rightly pointed out that he was one of the most talented of the 'new poets'.

According to K. R. S. Iyengar, 'To match is not a small achievement, to combine the current sophistication of linguistic finish with the old sophistication of romantic love' (1973, opt., cit., Asia Publishing House). Thus, A. K. Ramanujan is a genuine poet who had something worthwhile to say because he was the only one who knew how to say it, both in English and in his native tongue.

As we have reviewed, numerous poets are noted for their use of language, style, and craftsmanship. There seems to be an effort to develop their technique, as these poets learned, with some difficulty, to abandon styles inherited from others and attempt to recreate their own purposes.

Some of them preferred to write in traditional forms in the most convincing manner using free verse, trying to communicate their experiences through the flexibility of syntax and new uses of language. This gave rise to the hope of creating a new Indian English idiom. Hence, major poets of the 1960s marked the features of their own new Indian techniques, such as Kamla Das's elliptical style.

The sonorous style of O. P. Bhatnagar and the vigorous, deeply engaging style of Nissim Ezekiel are well noted. However, only A. K. Ramanujan and R. Parthasarathy were deeply concerned with the perfection of language. In this respect, A. K. Ramanujan, as well as R. Parthasarathy, was approximating Alexander Pope's attempts at perfecting language.

Nearly all critics, such as Pande S. N., Kurup, and Abidi, have pointed out his skill, diction, and craftsmanship. For instance, Lall R. states: "The terseness of his diction, the consummate skill with which he introduced rhyme and assonance into his verse, his sharply etched, crystallized images, and his disciplined handling of the English language made him one of the significant poets in India." (Opt. Cit., p. 95) As illustrated, A. K. Ramanujan's every poem possesses a unique and special quality. To appreciate and analyse a poem, this special quality arouses certain feelings and interpretations of the poet's intention. His use of simple, everyday words – apt and meaningful – helped him achieve Dantesque terseness and condensation.

His diction is notable for its epigrammatic terseness, felicity of expression, and classical simplicity and austerity. For instance, in his poem *Of Mothers, Among Other Things*, he writes: "Her saris do not cling; they hang loose feathers of a one-time wing." His use of monosyllabic words achieves a concentration of vowel sounds, which makes his diction musical. His use of rhyme and assonance further enhances the musical effect. Similarly, he employs an oblique, elliptical style, full of private insights, which allows him to juxtapose disparate elements.

Thus, his use of various stylistic devices conveys his meaning clearly, lucidly, eloquently, precisely, and accurately. Verbal irony is also considered an important aspect of his poetic diction, and *Obituary* is a fine example of this irony.

Throughout his poetic career, Ramanujan effectively uses the imagistic and ironic mode. He often employs sensuous, striking images, primarily for visual purposes, as seen in *Self-Portrait* and *Still Life*. However, his use of images in *Small Scale Reflection on Great House*, *Of Mothers, Among Other Things*, and the luminous evocations of family life in *Relation* are especially precise, accurate, real, and highly noticeable.

His imagery also creates vivid visual effects. The entire image of the spiritual evocation of the water bug in *The Striders* speaks to the poet's keen observation of details. He employs the ironic mode to introduce complexity, as seen in *Small Scale Reflections on a Great House*.

In this poem, he explores the relationship between his self-cantered house and the outside world. However, in *Prayers to Lord Murugan*, irony is used to deflate any religiosity associated with the poet's prayer. The ironic tone is employed for a satiric and mocking effect, which is also effectively used in his poems *History* and *Obituary*.

Similarly, we observe this effect in his poems *A River* and *Poona Train Window*. Additionally, his use of intelligent wordplay demonstrates his skilful use of irony to enhance meaning. For example, in the line, "O clockwork clicking in the silence within my walking," Ramanujan aims to achieve total detachment and impersonality. His objectivity is not merely an attitude but a conscious poetic strategy, as revealed in his short poems.

Thus, Ramanujan's poetry is symbolic and imagistic. His images are precise, accurate, simple, and highly suggestive. The luminous evocations of family life in *Relations*, especially in poems like *Small Scale Reflections on a Great House*, *Love Poem to a Wife I*, *Of Mothers, Among Other Things*, etc., are notable. His imagery creates vivid visual effects.

He prefers the concrete, the picturesque, and the precise over the general, the vague, and the abstract. In *The Striders*, for example, the insect is skilfully united with the divine and human elements. The vividly visualized imagery in *Snakes* and *Of Mothers, Among Other Things* deftly renders childhood memories through apt, precise, picturesque, and suggestive images.

Hence, his entire poetry is image-oriented. Although some of his poems are perfect in their use of imagery, his thought content is somewhat limited. The image takes precedence over thought. As a result, he works within a limited range of thought, seeking only those thoughts and feelings that can serve the image. Therefore, his poetry leaves a considerable area of thought unexplored. This fact also accounts for the relative thinness of his poetic output. To acclaim Ramanujan's artistry, the noted critic S. N. Pande quotes (2001, Atlantic Publishers, Opt. Cit)

> To clarify his vision, his artistry lies in his sensitive
>
> Use of language, which conceals the depth of his
>
> Thought and skillful use of themes

Thought, the poet yokes together the 'outer' and 'inner'

Forms of his mind and imagination by employing symbols

and images skillfully. Thus, it adds a new dimension

And colour to India and Indo English poetry. [5]

As a poet of society, he kept his eyes open to see what was going on around him. He drew his themes from anthropology, linguistics, folklore, religion, myth, meter, and logical structure to shape his experiences. Irony, paradox, and satire are effectively used, even in poems rooted in Hindu ethos. Thus, his craftsmanship in language and imagery never goes unnoticed. His innovation in language, theme, nostalgia, style, and technique produced unforgettable pieces of poetry. His interest in linguistics influenced him to conceptualize his poetry and poetic craftsmanship.

Although A. K. Ramanujan is often considered second to Nissim Ezekiel and as an expatriate poet from India, he never forgot his homeland, India. In fact, he proved that the secret of his success and his Indian-ness were major aspects of his poetry, marked by unmistakable authenticity of tone and treatment.

As a skilled translator, he translated Kannada and Tamil classics into English. To create a magic of words, he considered them as non-verbal content. He believed that words were like paint or gesture, or like objects – they have a sound, a look. He preferred language to say something new and innocent. He viewed the outside world as an aesthetic experience and considered himself the first reader. He also believed that a poet is a specialist.

As R. Parthasarathy said, the family is the central metaphor in Ramanujan's poetry, through which he explores his thoughts. The intricacies of family relationships have been a major theme, endlessly explored in Indian English poetry.

Though 'family' is the main metaphor in his poetry, Ramanujan views it within a historical context. He looks across an alien culture and a vast ocean to find his roots in Indian myth and tradition. The past constantly haunts his poetry. He does not construct his history from an unhistorical past; instead, he relates his personal and familial conflicts and frustrations to the Indian intellectual environment, both present and past. Thus, the theme of family helps us better understand his art.

Most of Ramanujan's poems originate from recollected personal emotions. They deal with the poet's memories of his relationships and the freedom that life away from them grants. For example, in his poem *Of Mothers, Among Other Things*, he remembers his intense love and sense of loss for his mother.

He vividly describes the great house closely related to his early life. In this poem, the poet recollects familial events and faces with which he was very intimate, making the entire description nostalgic. In his poem *History*, he exposes the greed within the family by narrating the incident of his aunt's death. His psychic drama, portrayed through the 'you' and 'I' conflict in *Love Poem for a Wife, I*, conveys the intensity of the poet's yearning for emotional fulfilment in familial relationships. A. K. Ramanujan's complete artistic detachment and irony portray the Indian scene from across the Atlantic, reflecting certain aspects of Indian-ness that have universal significance.

His adeptness in the use of irony in his poems is both visual and symbolic. For instance, in *Looking for a Cousin on a Swing*, the girl says that they were very innocent about riding and climbing a fig tree. Similarly, in *Still Another View of Grace*, he suggests that the old rag picker in Chicago, where he lived for three decades, could have been in Mysore. However, the irony in *A River* reveals that the river has enough water to be poetic about only once a year.

To highlight the self-deception of the Hindu, Ramanujan wrote poems on Hindu themes, such as *The Hindu: He Does Not Hurt a Fly*, *The Hindu: The Only Risk*, and *The Hindu: He Reads the Gita and is Calm at All Events*. His deep-rooted Hindu outlook is reflected in poems like *Obituary*, *Love Poem for a Wife, I*, and *Small-Scale Reflections on a Great House*.

As a Hindu, Ramanujan reacts strongly to certain aspects of Indian life and society, but his comments are never direct or explicit. His criticism is embedded in the way he designs and constructs images around themes such as sensation-loving poets, emperorship, and hypocritical societal figures. Hence, good-humoured irony pervades his work, as seen in *Self-Portrait*.

He also creates vivid poetic effects by deftly repeating a common phrase or word, which creates a haunting effect. The use of the same word both as a noun and a verb adds an ironic dimension. In *The Striders*, his tableau-like effect, vocabulary, and use of puns are also suggestive.

To conclude, the basic intention behind Ramanujan's use of language, style, and craftsmanship in his poetry was to capture the spirit of his characters in their actual form, thereby ensuring the reader's total participation. This approach also contributes to the creation of a new Indian English idiom through the study of his poetry. No doubt, Ramanujan was a skilled craftsman. His technical skill remains unmatched in Indian English poetry. His poetry reflects a specific culture, and his true poetic greatness lies in his ability to translate this experience into the terms of another culture. Hence, he used the English idiom with consummate skill and unmatched command. His image craft is unsurpassable. Thus, he is a flawless artist who sought perfection before publishing his work.

Although some of Ramanujan's poems are perfect in terms of image craft, his thought content is limited. The image takes precedence over thought, so he operates within a restricted range of ideas. He seeks only those thoughts and feelings that serve the image. As a result, his poetry leaves a considerable area of thought unexplored. This fact also accounts for the thinness of his poetic output.

The slenderness of his work can be attributed to his fastidiousness and meticulous attention to the aesthetic aspects of his poetry. His consummate artistry pushed him to strive for perfection before publishing any work. No doubt, we acknowledge his craftsmanship, even though there is no perfect rhythm present throughout his poetry. While he wrote with great skill, he lacks the same kind of quality we find in *Gitanjali* by Rabindranath Tagore or in prose by John Ruskin. Despite this, his poetry is acclaimed for its striking modernity and realism, though it does have its own limitations and weaknesses.

Almost all critics, both in India and abroad, have universally praised his poetry for its modernity and realism, particularly his 'detachment and impersonality,' which enhance the beauty of his work. However, in some poems, this detachment falters. In the case of his love poems, the complete detachment on the part of the poet is not necessarily a virtue. His treatment of the subject matter with such ruthless detachment requires a degree of emotional involvement. As a result, some critics consider his love poems contrived and insipid.

In fact, the mask of detachment in his poem *Obituary* can be irritating, as it distances the poet from his personal experience. However, the modulation of tone in the poem shifts, presenting a social picture through the obituary of his father in an intimate manner.

In the words of Burton Raffel, "It is nothing but a 'superfine objectivity,' illustrated in *The Striders* and *An Image for Politics*" (Pande,

S.N., 2001, Atlantic Publishers, Opt. Cit.). His poems *Snakes* and *Self Portrait* are quite effective, but the image in *Still Life* fails to carry the thematic weight. Therefore, Ramanujan uses only objective 'memory' in that poem. The role of memory in his poetry often reflects the loss of time, which can be described as a subjective memory. However, his use of objective memory in his poem *A River* connects the past and present, illustrating the notion of continuity.

At times, the images in his poetry are vague, incongruent, or excessively fanciful. For instance, the image of rain in *Of Mothers, Among Other Things* is described as vague by the critic S. Nagrajan. The image of the mother's hand as "two black pink crinkled feet" of a wet eagle is both fanciful and incongruent. In *The Striders*, the image of "dry capillary legs," as Burton Raffel points out, is scientifically sound but does not emerge from an authentic poetic experience. However, in his collection of unpublished poems, *The Black Hen*, Ramanujan confronts the present as it is.

At the end of this discussion, Indian writing in English faces two main problems. The first is the quality of experience that the poet wishes to express in English, and the second is the quality of the idiom the poet uses. In this context, one can effectively assess A. K. Ramanujan's poetry, as some of his poems demonstrate that he was able to overcome both of these challenges with ease and finesse. He successfully tackles a variety of themes in his work. Throughout his poetry, he manages to turn the ordinary into the exotic and the exotic into the ordinary, which is undoubtedly a unique achievement.

Overall, Ramanujan will remain in the minds of his readers for his innovativeness and for his use of language that, in a certain sense, was alien to him, yet retained an undeniably Indian essence. Ultimately, A. K. Ramanujan deserves high praise for his mastery of the English language and is rightly acclaimed as "the very Indian poet" among

Indo-Anglian writers because he brought something truly unique to the table.

The final section summarizes the earlier chapters, serving as a conclusion for each one, as proposed in the research methodology. The study was conducted with the aim of critically analysing Ramanujan's poetry. The structure of the chapters highlighted various aspects of his poetry, emphasizing his autobiographical and reflective nature. To establish him as a truly Indian expatriate poet and evaluate his poetic work, the research sought to uncover his distinctive qualities. The findings may vary based on the research strategy and design, but they ultimately synthesize the arguments and ideas presented in the preceding chapters. The conclusion is thus aligned with the research method.

The conclusion of this study aims to explore the principal reasons why almost every critic, both in India and abroad, has written about Indian English poetry, and why so many have taken special note of A. K. Ramanujan's work. This attention is not only due to his historical importance in the study of post-Independence Indian English poetry, but also because a reading of his poetry, from his first volume to his last, reveals the equal significance of both his original creative work and his translations. Therefore, it can be said that his poetry in English is imbued with a sensibility that is both distinctly Indian and Western in a unique way.

Thus, we accept his Indian sensibility and attempt to present his poetry from a balanced perspective, in order to clarify and evaluate him as both a poet and a creator of poetic works. His deep engagement with Indian-ness, despite his expatriate condition, makes his work fascinating and worthy of study. This book is a modest attempt to shed light on the remarkable contributions made by major poets like A. K. Ramanujan to Indian writing in English.

The primary goal of this study is to review the varied techniques employed by these poets to convey their vision of life. Furthermore, it aims to distinguish the distinctive features of their poetry, examining the symbolic significance of their works, moods, tones, and technical strategies that characterize contemporary Indian English poetry. In addition, this study has also sought to explore the emerging patterns of self-expression and the varied approaches to being a "new poet" within the Indian English tradition.

The primary objective of the present research is to critically study the poetry of A. K. Ramanujan, highlighting various aspects of his work, particularly his autobiographical nature. This study also emphasizes his identity as a truly Indian expatriate poet and a Hindu, as reflected both in his personal life and literary creations.

The research follows an explorative, interpretative, and descriptive approach, with each chapter addressing different facets of Ramanujan's poetry. This critical study evaluates his Indian identity and literary contributions from multiple perspectives, including psychological, nostalgic, existential, social, and cultural angles.

In presenting Ramanujan as an indigenous poet, this work focuses on his insights, particularly those rooted in autobiographical elements within his poetry. It also underscores his enterprising nature and deep Indian sensibility, which allowed him to connect with India's past, history, and tradition in a unique way. Therefore, it can be concluded that Ramanujan made a significant breakthrough by cross-fertilizing English with native literary traditions, earning him recognition as a polyglot writer, a critic, and a distinguished literary figure.

Overall, this book provides a critical study of the literary contributions of A. K. Ramanujan, presented across six chapters. The work begins with an 'Abstract,' followed by a comprehensive survey of the pre- and post-Independence period, offering a critical evaluation of both major and minor poets, highlighting their exceptional gifts and individual talents.

The book then examines the complex nature of life, focusing on Ramanujan's creative perception and exploring the major themes in his poetry, such as mysticism, metaphysical longing, spirituality, and philosophical concerns. This section delves into both his personal life and literary contributions.

Ramanujan's creative vision is explored in depth, demonstrating the psychological realism and variety present in his work. The book further traces his development as a poet, acknowledging his contributions to Indian English literature and the significance of his literary achievements as a whole.

Thus, we come to appreciate through appreciation and enjoy through enjoyment, where the end and the means are inseparable. As a modern and intellectual poet, A. K. Ramanujan refined his critical idiom, drawing influences from diverse sources, including intellectual, philosophical, and psychological realms.

In this chapter, an attempt has been made to explore various aspects of Ramanujan as a literary figure, poet, critic, and his poetry in general. It provides valuable insights for studying this book, highlighting his masterful poetic craftsmanship and offering an integrated view of various critical perspectives. Ultimately, the chapter concludes by summarizing the findings of the book and encapsulating the key arguments, ideas, and conclusions from the earlier sections.

Bibliography

{References with Endnotes}

A) Primary - Sources

I) Principal Sources:

1) Volumes:

- The Striders, 1966, Vol. I
- Relations, 1971, Vol. I
- Selected Poems, 1976, Vol. III
- Second Sight, 1986, Vol. IV
- (The Black Hen, unpublished) included in the collected poems, 1995, New Delhi: Oxford
- The Collected Essays (Prose), 1999, New Delhi

2) Translations:

- Fifteen Poems from a Classical Tamil Anthology, 1967
- The Interior Landscape: Love Poems
- Speaking of Siva, 1973, Harmondsworth: Penguin
- Samskara: A Rite for a Dead Man by U. R. Anantha-murthy
- Hymns for the Drowning: Poems for Vishnu by Nammalvar, 1986, Princeton Univ. Press
- The - Ten Long Poems of Classical Tamil, 1985
- Folktales from India: A Selection of Oral
- Tales from Twentieth Languages, 1991, New York

3) Journals & Periodicals:

- Indian Literature, Ind. Writing in English (V)
- Sahitya Academi's Bi-monthly Journal

- Indian Writing in English by, Balramgupta
- Bi-monthly Journal by M. Bhatnagar

4) Periodicals:

- N B T Newsletter, Sultanchand Book, Macmillan New Books
- B. R. World of Books, A F Books, Publisher's Profile etc.

B) Secondary - Sources

1) Books and Dissertations:

Abidi, S. Z. H., "Studies in Indo-Anglian Poetry", 1996, Prakash Book Depot.

Bhatnagar Manmohan K. / Rajeshwar. (Ed.), Vol.VI, "Indian Writing in English", Atlantic Publishers, 2001.

Bhatnagar Manmohan K. / Rajeshwar. (Ed.), Vol.I to X, Vol. I, II, III, IV, V, VI, VII, VIII. Shahane V.A., "Indian Poetry in English: A Critical Assessment", Macmillan, 1980.

Bhatnagar O.P., The Indian Poetry in English: The Contemporary Situation", 1980.

Dr. Das, B.K., "Aspects of Modern Indian Poetry in English", the Indian Journal of English Studies, 1980.

Dr.Das B.K., "Review of Ten Twentieth Century Indian Poets", Prakash Book Depot, 1993.

Dwivedi, A.N., "A.K. Ramanujan and His Poetry" ,N.D: Dooba House

Dwivedi, A.N., 1982, "The Poetry of A.K. Ramanujan: Cultural Ambivalence and Personal Dilemma".

Dwivedi, A.N., "Second Sight: Indian ness of A.K. Ramanujan's Poetry", Indian Literature.

Dharwadkar, Vinay., 1994, "A. K. Ramanujan: Author, Translator, Scholar", World Lit. Today

Daruwalla, K.N., "Two Decades of Indian Poetry", 1960-80, New Delhi: Vikas Publishing House, 1980.

Ezekiel, Nissim, "Two Poets: A.K. Ramanujan and Keki N. Daruwalla", the Illustrated Weekly of India, Vol. 93, 1972 ,

Gokak, V.K., "Golden Treasury of Indian English Poetry".

Gokak, V.K., (Ed.), "The Golden Treasury of Indo-Anglian Poetry", New Delhi: Sahitya Akademi, 1986.

Harrex, S.C., "Small Scale Reflections on Indian English Poetry", the Journal of Indian Writing in English, 1980.

Iyengar, K.R.S., "Indian Writing in English", Bombay: Asia Publishing House, 1973.

Jha, Rama, 1981, "A Conversation with A.K. Ramanujan", Humanities Press.

Jussawalla, Adil, "The New Poetry", Journal of Commonwealth Literature, No. 5, 1967.

Kurup, P.K.J., "Contemporary Indian Poetry in English", Atlantic Publishers, 1996.

King, Bruce, "Modern Indian Poetry in English

King, Bruce, "Three Indian Poets King,

King, Bruce. (Ed.), "Literature of the World in English", London: Routelege and Kegan Paul, 1974.

Kulshrestha, Chirantan, "The Self in Ramanujan's Poetry", The Indian Journal of English Studies, Vol. 17

Kumar Satish / Tayal, "Selected Poems".

Kulshrestha, Chirantan., (Ed., "Contemporary Indian English Verse: An Evaluation", 1980.

Kurup, P.K.J., "The Self in the Poetry of A.K. Ramanujan", Contemporary Indian Poetry in English, New Delhi: Atlantic Publishers, 1991.

Lall, Ramji, "Indo-Anglian Poetry", R.B., 2002.

Mirza, Taqi Ali, 1980, "A.K. Ramanujan's Particular Hell", 1980.

Naik M.K., "Aspects in Indian Writing in English", Madras: Macmillan, 1982.

Nagarjan, S., "A. K. Ramanujan", Quest, No. 74, 1972.

Naik, M. K., "A. K. Ramanujan and the Search for Roots", the Humanities Review, Vol. 3: 1981.

Naik M.K., (Ed.), "Perspectives on Indian Poetry in English", New Delhi: Abhinav Publication, 1981

Nandi, Pritish, (Ed.), "Indian Poetry ion English To day", New Delhi: Sterling Publishers, Private Limited, 1981

Pande, S. N. 2001, "Millennium Perspectives on A.K.Ramanujan", Atlantic Publishers, 2001

Panikar, K. A., "Four Voices and a Medium", Indian Book Chronicle, Vol.2: No. 11, 1977.

Parthsarthy, R., (Ed.), "Ten Twentieth Century Indian Poets", 1976, Oxford Univ. Press.

Parthasarthy, R., 1976, "How It Strikes a Contemporary: The Poetry of A.K. Ramanujan", 1976.

Pal, K. S., "Ramanujan-Ezekiel: A Comparative Study", Parthasarthy, R., "Ten Twentieth Century Indian Poets", Delhi: O.U.P., 1994.

Parthasarthy, R., "How It Strikes a Contemporary: The Poetry of A.K. Ramanujan". In The Literary Creation, Vol. XIII, 1976

Ramamurti, K.S., "Twenty Five Indian Poets in English", Macmillan, 1995

Rao, Raghvendra, "Reverse Romantism: The Case of A.K. Ramanujan's 'The Striders' ".

Rao, K.R., (Ed.), "Reverse Romanticism", 1979

Shahane V.A., "Indian Poetry in English: A Critical Assessment", Macmillan, 1980.

Singh, Kirpal., "A.K.Ramanujan / the Poet", 1999, Literature Series / 6, 5, 4, Vrinda Publications.

Singh, Satyanarain., "Ramanujan and Ezekiel", Usmania Journal of English Studies, Vol.7, 1969.

Sivamkrishna, M., "Contemporary Indian Poetry in English: An Approach", Opinion Literary Quarterly, Vol. I: No. 4, 1974.

Sarang, Vilas. (Ed.), "Indian English Poetry since 1950: An Anthology", Bombay: Disha Books, 1999.

Tilak, R., "New Indian English Poets and Poetry", R.B., 2001

Vergheese, C. Paul, "Problems of the Indian Creative Writer in English", Bombay: Somaiya Publications, 1971.

Williams, H.M., "Indo-Anglian Literature", 1800-1970

About the Author

"**A. K. Ramanujan's Search for Creativity**" is an entitled edited Book written with a view to study it critically. It aimed at to highlight and signify A.K. Ramanujan as a truly Indian expatriate poet and a Hindu by both of his literary and personal point of view. Here, my editorial purpose is to prove A. K. Ramanujan's search for his Creativity as an editor in my Book.

At present, **Dr. Kulkarni Sanjay G**. is working as an Associate-Professor-in-English at ABSS' N. S. B. College, Nanded since last fifteen years at U. G. level College. He is a distinguished research person, academic writer and resource supervisor till today. His area of thrust is Indian Writing in English. He has contributed extensively to different Journals and Publications. He has to his credit the best three books and eleven research papers.

(Address information details are for you only Sir ji)

A) Official Address: Dr. Kulkarni Sanjay G.
Associate Professor, Department of English,
ABSS' N.S.B. College, Tarasingh Market,
Nanded-431602
(Maharashtra State)

B) Personal Address: Shri. Sanjay Ganpatrao Kulkarni
Row House No. E-1/18, "Chaitanya Nivas"
Gut. No.228; Plot No.18, Near 'Ram Bag,'
Kautha, Nanded-431605 (Maharashtra State)

C) Communication Address:
Contact Mob. No.   i) {9420073284}
{Sanjay G. Kulkarni}
Email. Id -   sgknsb@gmail.com
OR
Contact No.   ii) {918830734695}
{Samruddhi Sanjay Kulkarni}
Email. Id -   samruddhi.kulkarni009@gmail.com